NORTH
DAKOTA
BEER

NORTH DAKOTA BEER

A HEADY HISTORY

ALICIA UNDERLEE NELSON

AMERICAN PALATE

Published by American Palate

A Division of The History Press

Charleston, SC

www.historypress.net

Cover image of North Dakota's Theodore Roosevelt National Park and the curving Little
Missouri River, courtesy of goodfreephotos.com.

First published 2017

Manufactured in the United States

ISBN 9781625859198

Library of Congress Control Number: 2017934938

To the unsung heroes: The storytellers, librarians, historians, collectors, journal writers, curators and ordinary people who preserve and tend stories so the rest of us can read them.

To my Eli: Everything I do is for you.

CONTENTS

ACKNOWLEDGEMENTS

Thank you to my parents, Wayne and Christy, for supporting my work and encouraging my imagination since the days I wrote my stories in crayon.

Thanks also to my husband, Derrick, for pulling my weight while I typed furiously at all hours of the night and for putting up with an endless stream of beer and historical trivia. I appreciate your support so much.

Love to my sweet boy, Eli, for forcing your creative, unstructured mama to arrange her day in twenty-minute increments, which made me more efficient than anyone could have predicted.

Thanks to my brother, Jacob Underlee; Sarah Hinnenkamp; and Joe Baur for being my first readers.

Cheers to the brewers in these pages, past and present. Thanks for the great beer and fantastic stories.

A hearty thank-you to every maltster, vendor, neighbor and farmer I talked to. You bring these stories to life.

Special thanks to Aaron Juhnke of Junkyard Brewing Company, Frank Clemens of Flatland Brewery and Mark Bjornstad of Drekker Brewing Company for helping me translate brewing history and techniques.

Thanks to JoRelle Grover and Joseph Steinmann for translating my words into images.

Much appreciation to the staff at the Old Broadway and Granite City Food and Brewery for kick-starting my on-the-job beer education and to the guys of Fargo Brewing Company for once hiring me to write about their beer.

Thank you to Katie Belgarde and Eli Baana for the spontaneous technical support.

Many thanks to Royce Granlund for sharing your Dakota Beer memorabilia with me.

And last, a huge thank-you to Mark Peihl and Markus Krueger of the Historical and Cultural Society of Clay County and the late Frank Vyzralek of the State Historical Society of North Dakota. This book builds on your excellent work and would not have been possible without it.

INTRODUCTION

North Dakotans love beer. And we drink an awful lot of it. According to a Beer Marketer's Insights poll, residents of North Dakota consumed 43.6 gallons of beer per adult of legal drinking age in 2013, the most of any state in the nation.

Today is a very good day to be a beer fan in North Dakota. You can sit on a barstool and sip locally brewed red ale on the edge of the North Dakota badlands, a landscape that feels as untamed now as it did when Native American hunters and traders ruled the region. You can ask a brewer about the local malt he used in his pale ale or sample a wide range of beers, from esoteric sours to silky, smooth porters at communal taproom tables from Minot to Mandan. Taprooms and brewpubs have emerged in revitalized city centers, no-frills industrial parks, busy shopping districts and sleepy subdivisions, giving an increasingly diverse and beer-savvy population a place to drink local, right in the neighborhood.

This wasn't always the case. When I moved to North Dakota and started bartending at the Old Broadway in downtown Fargo in 2002, the most exotic beer on tap was Guinness. The fact that one of my regulars had to teach me a proper Guinness pour is a pretty good illustration of how few people ordered it. Fargo was a lager kind of town in a light beer state. The very bar I worked in had once been a brewpub, but I missed it (and what I now know was the second North Dakota beer boom) by just a few years. Thankfully, I was just in time for the next one.

I've been lucky enough to have a front-row seat for North Dakota's craft beer renaissance. I first got into beer as a cocktail server and bartender. Now I'm the girl in the taproom with a notebook, the one with her camera out, taking eighteen shots of my flight because the thin dew of condensation on the glasses is just so darn pretty. I'm the weird one who walks up to your table and asks what you're drinking and if I should try it. I know I've found a fellow beer nerd when I get a grin and a torrent of recommendations instead of the usual polite North Dakota smile.

My colleague Jack Dura, who contributed a photo to this book, once jokingly told me that there are only two degrees of separation between North Dakotans, instead of the agreed-on six degrees of separation that apply to the rest of the world and to Kevin Bacon party games. You don't need to carry a reporter's notebook to know this is true. Our population is growing, but our borders still contain fewer than 760,000 people, all of whom share one area code. We support our own.

I think that there might only be one degree of separation between North Dakota beer enthusiasts. And thank God for that. I couldn't have written this story without the brewers, beer nerds, maltsters, homebrewers, vendors and farmers of North Dakota. The book's nuances and much of its self-deprecating sense of humor (an underrated North Dakota trait) come as much from them as they do from me. The wildest stories, however, come almost entirely from the settlers who migrated to this place. Don't ever let anyone tell you that history is boring. The first generations of these prairie people threw some epic parties and could probably drink us all under the table.

We don't like to brag in this part of the country (it's not nice, dontcha know), and we give the side eye to anyone who thinks too much of themselves. But North Dakota has contributed some pretty great beer and some awfully tall tales to the craft beer canon. And the story of North Dakota's craft beer resurgence is still being written as the industry evolves.

Our state may never have as many breweries as some of the big craft brewing states, and we're completely okay with that. Comparing ourselves to other places has never been our style. We're building North Dakota beer by ourselves, for ourselves, from farm field to brewery to table, one pint at a time. It's been working pretty well so far. And there's more good stuff to come.

Cheers!

Chapter I

COMMON ALE, ENLISTED MEN AND HURDY-GURDY GIRLS

Worlds Collide in Dakota Territory, 1738-1871

They who drink beer will think beer.
—Washington Irving

North Dakota beer was local before local was cool. Brewers were commercially producing beer two decades before North Dakota became a state, and farmers in the region have grown barley and hops since the 1870s.

The people of North Dakota have been beer fans since white settlers arrived on the scene. The region had a reputation for hard partying and all-night, shoot-'em-up dance parties in its earliest days as a U.S. territory. North Dakotans just kept on dancing, drinking and brewing their own beer right through the state's lengthy prohibition period and into the modern craft beer renaissance with little regard for laws and regulations.

They didn't just brew their own—they grew their own, too. Before statehood, local farmers sold barley to be made into beer directly to brewers and maltsters. The state has been among the top three barley producers in the nation since the 1930s, and North Dakota farmers now supply barley to brewers across the country.

Fort Totten. *Alicia Underlee Nelson.*

NORTH DAKOTA'S FIRST BEER

North Dakota's first beer review on record comes from Fort Totten, a frontier fort tasked with monitoring the mail and supply routes between Minneapolis/St. Paul and Montana. This rural outpost was located in the north-central part of Dakota Territory, near what is now Devils Lake. On New Year's Eve 1868, assistant surgeon J.N.T. King took a sip of "common ale" from the small brewery overseen by the fort's sutler, Ernest Brenner.

King was *not* impressed. "It is a miserable article & not fit to drink. There is little taste of beer, hops or malt about it," King wrote in his diary. Either Brenner, a German immigrant, didn't inherit his countrymen's knack for brewing (in all fairness, he immigrated to Boston as a kid) or he made a mistake during the brewing process. Or maybe King was the territory's first beer snob.

Clearly, Brenner's "common ale" didn't impress its first critic. But the first brewer on record in what is now North Dakota probably made ale his flagship beer for very practical reasons. First, ale was popular and accessible. It had been a common drink among white settlers in the United States since colonization. It held some nutritional value, had a low percentage of alcohol by volume (ABV) and was often safer to drink than the local water, so everyone (even children and pregnant women) drank it regularly. It was served at meals and considered a table beer.

Many families brewed their own beer at home. Ale doesn't require cold storage during the brewing process, so homebrewers and sutlers (merchants who sold supplies to soldiers) like Brenner wouldn't have needed to cut blocks of ice from nearby rivers or lakes to keep it cold or sacrifice valuable cellar space to store it.

Brewing Beer

Brenner and other brewers of his day would likely have malted their own barley by soaking the grain in a bucket to start the germination process. Once the individual grains of barley began to float, they were skimmed off the top, dried, rinsed in clean water and dried again. Brewery staff spread the grains out on a flat surface (often the brewery floor) and turned the grain with a shovel or another tool so the barley would dry evenly, maintain a consistent temperature and wouldn't mold. This malted barley was made into beer using a process that hasn't changed much over the centuries.

The brewer soaks the malted barley in water to separate the grain's proteins from its sugars. This process creates a sweet, sugary liquid called wort (pronounced "wert"). The wort is boiled in a kettle with hops—the dried, female flowers harvested from a hop plant.

The cone-like flowers of the hop plant grow on climbing bines (not vines—they don't have the little tendrils that pull themselves up, like cucumbers do). Hops are perennial plants that are native to the 48th parallel north, a band that stretches across the globe and includes beer-brewing hot spots like Germany and the U.S. Pacific Northwest, as well as—you guessed it—the land that would soon become North Dakota.

When boiled, hops impart a bitter flavor to balance the wort's sweetness, enhance a beer's aroma and help stabilize and preserve the beer. They also have antibacterial properties that inhibit bacteria growth but allow the yeast, which is added next, to thrive.

This yeast converts the water, hops and barley into beer by fermenting the sugars in the wort and releasing CO_2. Brewers, both then and now, use two different strains of yeast when they're making beer: top-fermenting strains and bottom-fermenting strains.

Ales like Brenner's would have used a top-fermenting yeast that works best at brewing temperatures between fifty-three and seventy-seven degrees Fahrenheit. Just like the name suggests, these yeasts rise to the top of the kettle during fermentation. Top-fermenting yeasts were used in the most popular beers in America during the Civil War period, including ales like the one brewed at Fort Totten. They're also used to make porters and stouts and older European varieties like wheat beers, altbier and kölsch.

Bottom-fermenting strains are used during a colder fermentation process, between forty-four and fifty-nine degrees Fahrenheit. As the name suggests, the yeast settles to the bottom during fermentation. These yeasts are used in the crisp, easy-drinking lagers that would become very popular in the United States as cold brewing and cold storage options improved in the 1870s, as well as straw-colored, Bohemian pilsners and the pale lagers and medium-bodied, amber-hued märzenbiers from Germany.

A North Dakota Beer Breakdown

Brenner grew up in the United States, but the beer his parents knew back in the old country would have been made under the principles of the *Reinheitsgebot*, Duke William (Wilhelm) IV of Bavaria's 1516 beer purity law that decreed that only beverages brewed with water, barley and hops (and later yeast) can be called beer in Germany. Since Bavaria had been a beer-brewing leader for centuries, this decree influenced the way beer was brewed all over the world.

If Brenner brewed Fort Totten's "common ale" according to *Reinheitsgebot* methods, the bland result that King tasted could have indicated a brewing mistake, like improper malting or the introduction of bacteria during the fermentation process. Brenner may not have boiled the hops long enough to extract their full flavor. The barley kernels may have yielded very little extractable malt. He may have intentionally made a very mellow beer. Or maybe King just wasn't into it.

It's also possible that King didn't detect the flavor of hops in Brenner's ale because the brewer didn't actually use any. Unlike beer made under the German purity law and most modern beers, many early American ale recipes didn't call for hops at all. Commercial brewers of Brenner's era and the first U.S. homebrewers often made a sweet, full-bodied, amber-colored brew using just three ingredients—water, malt and yeast.

The fort's remote location may have made sourcing hops a challenge. Hops grow wild in North Dakota, but Brenner may not have known where to locate them. Even if he found enough wild hops to brew, we don't know enough about the flavor profile of native North Dakota hops to guess how they would have influenced his beer.

Buying hops at a good price and transporting them to the fort's remote location would have been tricky, too. A series of crop failures at hop yards in New York just after the end of the Civil War caused a massive shortage and a 700 percent increase in hop prices. Enterprising farmers in nearby Wisconsin jumped on the hops bandwagon and led the nation in hops production until 1870, when the industry shifted to and remained centered in the Pacific Northwest.

Fort Totten wasn't served by the steamboats carrying cargo along the Red River of the North (which would become the eastern border of North Dakota) or the Missouri River to the west, so Brenner had to travel overland for supplies. He would have gone east (most often to Minnesota's capital, St. Paul, or Minneapolis, its sister city) just a few times a year. Expensive hops might have been low on his priority list.

INSIDE THE FIRST NORTH DAKOTA BREWERY

We don't know precisely how Brenner brewed, but we do know a little bit about his brewhouse. According to *A Bicentennial History of Devils Lake, North Dakota*, both Brenner's store and the brewery were "maintained in rough log structures, the brewery building containing three rooms or apartments.... The apparatus for the brewery consisted of a great kettle, a mess tub, and a cooling tank. Ten barrels of beer could be brewed at a time. The brewing process took several days and generally occurred once a week."

Each barrel Brenner brewed would have held 31 gallons of beer. Abraham Lincoln's administration effectively standardized the size of a barrel in 1862 when it enacted the one-dollar excise tax on every 31-gallon barrel of beer to finance the U.S. Civil War. The modern half-barrel keg holds exactly half that amount: 15.5 gallons.

Brewers still measure their output in barrels. So, if the records show that a brewery produced 1,000 barrels of beer annually, that means it brewed 2,000 half-barrel kegs.

BREWING AND DRINKING BEER AT FORT ABERCROMBIE

Fort Abercrombie, the first military installation in what would become North Dakota, also had a brewery on site. It was a low, rough-hewn log structure that resembled the other buildings on the fort's grounds.

Built in 1858 along the west bank of the Red River, Fort Abercrombie was heralded as the "Gateway to the West." Its remote prairie location near present-day Wahpeton (about half an hour's drive south of Fargo) was perfect for keeping an eye on the brand-new state of Minnesota just across the river and monitoring the mail and supply routes in the area. Some of those routes reached northwest to Fort Totten and on to other frontier forts in the region.

Unlike Fort Totten, Fort Abercrombie benefited from regular deliveries of supplies and mail. Fort Abercrombie was located along an ox-cart (and eventually stagecoach) trail between St. Paul and Fort Garry, where the Assiniboine and Red Rivers meet in what is now downtown Winnipeg, Manitoba. The steamships followed a similar route north along the Red

The brewery at Fort Abercrombie. *State Historical Society of North Dakota (SHSND), A2007-00001.*

River, docking at Fort Abercrombie to distribute the region's mail and other cargo before moving north.

The sutler—and probable brewer—at Fort Abercrombie was David McCauley. When McCauley wasn't selling supplies (or presumably brewing the ale the fort produced), he delivered the mail and established a village (the not-so-cleverly named McCauleyville) that became the first white settlement in the southern Red River Valley. It was built on the Minnesota side of the Red River and was the first of a handful of border cities that would serve thirsty beer fans from the land that would become North Dakota.

Life at a remote fort was notoriously boring, so soldiers passed the time between drills and their work details playing cards, gambling and drinking whatever they could get their hands on, according to Don Rickey Jr., who wrote about frontier fort shenanigans in his book *Forty Miles a Day on Beans and Hay: The Enlisted Soldier Fighting the Indian Wars*: "Beer was always a favored beverage. It was customarily sold in quart bottles packed in straw-filled barrels. Post traders and sutlers generally charged fifty cents to one dollar for a quart of beer; later the post canteens sold it at the lower price of eighteen to fifty cents a quart."

A soldier's thirty-two-ounce bottle would have dwarfed a modern twelve-ounce bottle and could fill a pint glass (which has a capacity of sixteen fluid ounces) twice. So, when soldiers wrote in their journals about having a few beers, it's worth noting that just one of their beers was at least twice the size of a beer today.

"Although some drank little or not at all, large numbers were accustomed to heavy drinking, and many spent most of their pay for beer and whisky," explained Rickey. "The army's general attitude was one of tolerance, because officers realized liquor provided an escape or, at least, an artificial and temporary amelioration of the dull, hard and lonely lives of men."

The First Beer Imports

If a pioneer fort didn't have a brewery on site, the steamships' cargo often included beer for the soldiers, including varieties that the brewers at Fort Totten and Fort Abercrombie weren't making. Excavations near Fort Rice, which housed soldiers south of Mandan from 1864 to 1878, unearthed shards of ceramic and glass bottles that contained both stout and ale. They were very similar to bottles found in the wreck of a steamboat that sank in

Soldiers drinking beer at Fort Lincoln, near Mandan. *State Historical Society of North Dakota (SHSND), A1080.*

1865 near Omaha, Nebraska, that were sealed with cork and held in place with a wire cage.

Bottles from the same era were found at Fort Buford, which was built at the confluence of the Yellowstone and Missouri Rivers near the present-day Montana border in 1866. Like the soldiers at Fort Rice, the men at Fort Buford also drank stout, a beer brewed at high heat and made with barley that's roasted before it's malted, creating a rich taste and a distinctly dark color.

THE BEER SCENE AT FRONTIER FORTS

Officers and the enlisted men drank and socialized in separate quarters, except for holidays, where schedules were relaxed and the entire fort celebrated together. Sometimes they celebrated with beer.

The garrison at Fort Rice celebrated the Christmas of 1868 with a German shindig. Surgeon Washington Matthews's December 24, 1868 diary entry notes that "a number of enlisted Germans having formed a German [singing] Society at the post, their first entertainment was given this Christmas Eve. It consisted of songs and supper and the drinking of a weak, home-made beer. The officers of the Fort were all invited."

We don't know who made this early "home-made" beer. The sutler or cook would have had space to brew and access to supplies. It's also possible that a fort with enough enlisted German immigrants to form a German singing group might also have enough enlisted Germans to create a decent beer. This diary entry may be the state's first recorded mention of homebrewing, a tradition that would supply North Dakota drinkers with beer even in the face of prohibition. Like the singers at Fort Rice, many of the state's most prolific homebrewers had German ancestry.

The parties at Fort Abercrombie could get a little wilder than the Fort Rice Christmas party. All the cool kids in the 1850s and 1860s were into fiddle music, so the soldiers must have been pumped when they learned that two fiddlers would play at "Sandy's Ball," a bash hosted and catered by Sandy, Fort Abercrombie's Scottish cook.

The party got off to a roaring start, according to Augustus Meyers, who wrote about it in *Ten Years in the Ranks: U.S. Army*. Sandy set out bottles of ale from the Fort Abercrombie brewery, whiskey punch and champagne. The tables were heaped with ham, sardines and pickles on stone china dishes purchased in St. Paul for the occasion.

Everyone was drinking and dancing until a series of brawls sent the party into overdrive. The fiddlers bickered over the set list, an argument that ended when one smashed his instrument over his partner's head and was tossed out. Around midnight, the soldiers got testy, and bottles and plates started flying. When Sandy got up on a table and begged everybody to be careful with his china, they tipped the table over, dishes and all.

Maybe the party would have gone differently if there were more than just a handful of women in attendance, a guest list limitation that forced the guys to get cozy on the dance floor with their fellow soldiers. Yep, you read that right. This party, like pretty much every party for enlisted men on the frontier, was a total dude fest.

The soldiers' remote location and regimented lives gave them very few chances to get friendly with the ladies. They lived and worked apart from women who had business at the forts, like female fur trappers (who usually arrived with husbands in tow) or the fort laundresses, and mingling wasn't allowed. The very few eligible young women in the area were shielded from a soldier's advances, since the young, low-status enlisted men weren't members of the brand-new white settler communities or the more established fur trading society in the region.

While this was clearly an issue for the guys for personal reasons, it also really messed up the vibe at their dance parties. What's a dance-loving soldier to do when most of the best dances are designed to be danced in pairs? "Simple," the enlisted men across the nation decided, "We'll just hold stag dances and take turns being the girls. Problem solved!"

And they did. The designated "ladies" dressed as women, wore white cloth bands on their arms or carried handkerchiefs and danced the women's parts. There were several soldiers dancing with men wearing ladies' clothing at "Sandy's Ball." Nobody seemed to think this was at all odd (or perhaps a *tad* homoerotic). Either the men at these forts were pretty darn secure in their masculinity or whatever happened on the frontier stayed on the frontier.

The men at Fort Abercrombie were luckier than most. They could cross the Red River and walk to McCauleyville, near what is now Kent, Minnesota. David McCauley's town is just a sleepy cluster of houses now, but back then, it was home to seven saloons and a hurdy-gurdy house.

Dancing the Hurdy-Gurdy

After long nights of getting drunk on ale and dancing with their buddies, even the plainest girl in the McCauleyville hurdy-gurdy house must have looked like a knockout. She would have been dressed to kill in flirty, cleavage-baring dresses, with her skirts hemmed scandalously high to show off her calves and her kicky kid boots. A hurdy-gurdy girl (called a "hurdy-gurdy," or just a "hurdy" for short) wasn't a prostitute, but she wasn't exactly an innocent either. She was a musician, hired to entertain and charm the men on the frontier.

The joints got their name from the instrument the girls played. A hurdy-gurdy is a stringed instrument that's played by continuously rotating a wheel with a hand crank that activates the strings. (It sounds a lot like a bagpipe.) The music was lively and often German. So were most of the women.

The accepted hurdy-gurdy girl origin story is that German farmers (who had served the British as soldiers for hire) discovered that they sold more brooms at the market when music and pretty girls were present. A few enterprising businessmen added alcohol to the mix and offered impoverished female musicians passage to frontier America and the mining regions of Australia in exchange for a hurdy-gurdy gig.

It sounds like a page right out of a sex trafficker's handbook, but the women weren't allowed to engage in sexual activity. This odd form of dance hall indentured servitude placed German women in gold rush towns across the United States and in pioneer settlements like the one near Fort Abercrombie.

The hurdies sold dances in five- to fifteen-minute increments for fifty to seventy-five cents each. The patrons could also purchase packages that included dances and drinks for himself and his partner. The performer split the profits with the house. A good hurdy-gurdy could book fifty dances a night and was protected as the valuable asset she was.

A team of chaperones (usually a married couple) stayed with the women continuously. The bartenders helped, too. They served the men the drinks they paid for but gave the women weak tea or colored water instead of the whiskey or beer the men bought them, since nobody could drink dozens of drinks and keep dancing and playing all night.

The women dancing with the soldiers in the Red River Valley were among the very last generation of hurdy-gurdy girls. The German government thought the whole business was a little creepy and passed laws limiting the export of performers in 1865. It didn't take long for the performers to age out of a profession that prized youth and beauty. Since they hadn't been sex workers, hurdy-gurdies integrated back into mainstream life in the United States or Germany fairly easily, often paying off their debts, marrying and raising families.

WHY BEER CAME TO THE PRAIRIE

Beer arrived in North Dakota with the U.S. Army. The presence of soldiers at frontier forts like Fort Abercrombie, Fort Rice and Fort Totten was just one of many changes that would completely disrupt existing land use practices, trade alliances and beliefs about alcohol in the region.

See, the land that was to become North Dakota wasn't exactly the empty frontier that newspaper ads at the time made it out to be. The Mandan, Hidatsa, Arikara, Chippewa, Sioux and Assiniboine nations have been living, working, farming, hunting and trading here for thousands of years. But since the tribes of the Great Plains had no tradition of drinking alcohol before contact with white fur traders (*voyageurs*) in the eighteenth century, most of their history falls outside the scope of a book about beer. Tribal members were the original teetotalers in a state that has a long history of tension between heavy drinkers and those who abstain.

The arrival of hard-drinking explorers and soldiers was just one of the many challenges North Dakota's most established societies would encounter after the first white *voyageur* appeared in a Mandan village in 1738. New trading partnerships were formed with *voyageurs* and fur trading companies, and steamboats offered expanded trade routes. But the same partnerships that brought trade also brought deadly diseases. Later, treaties between the U.S. government and Native American leaders redrew the map of the land that would become North Dakota. Railroads replaced rivers and ox-cart trails as the major conduits for trade, which influenced settlement patterns, business development and even local liquor laws.

NORTH DAKOTA'S FIRST COMMUNITIES

North Dakota has been a booming agricultural and trade center for centuries. Mandan, Arikara (who called themselves Sahnish) and Hidatsa (who knew themselves as Minnetaree) nations operated bustling earth lodge villages, farms and trading posts along the banks of the Knife and Missouri Rivers in what's now the central part of the state. The women and girls (yes, North Dakota's first farmers were female) grew corn, squash, beans and other crops along the fertile riverbanks. Their crops were traded for goods from around the world.

The people who lived and hunted in what is now North Dakota's northeastern quadrant, where their territory stretched into the land that became Manitoba and Minnesota, called themselves Ojibwe. The settlers they encountered called them Chippewa. Pembina, a community of traders and trappers in this region, just south of what's now the Manitoba border, was said to be the first permanent white settlement in what is now North Dakota. In reality, there were people of many nations living near the fur trading post in Pembina, including Chippewa, Cree, French-Canadian, English, American and Métis, the children of white *voyageurs* and their Native American wives.

The Sioux nation (Oceti Šakowiŋ) includes seven tribes who lived and hunted in the southern and western portions of what is now North Dakota and farther south into modern South Dakota and east into what's now Minnesota. Tribal members spoke three related Siouan dialects, Dakota, Nakota and Lakota. North Dakota draws its name from a Siouan word that means "friendly" or "allied."

The American Fur Company built Fort Union in 1828 at the request of the Assiniboine nation, whose members lived near the present Montana and Saskatchewan borders. They called themselves Nakota or Nakoda. (Sound familiar? The Assiniboine also speak a Siouan language.) Fort Union was located near the confluence of the Yellowstone and Missouri Rivers, steps from the modern North Dakota and Montana border. It wasn't a military outpost but rather a private enterprise that did an average of $100,000 in annual business.

The End of an Era

Inspired by the success of Fort Union, the American Fur Company built Fort Clark on the Missouri River northwest of modern Bismarck in 1830 and 1831. The first steamboat in what's now North Dakota docked there in 1832.

It was business as usual when a steamboat docked at Fort Clark on June 18, 1837. But the contents of this particular ship also included passengers with smallpox. Every tribe in the region had been hit by disease outbreaks since the first contact with Europeans, but they'd never seen anything like this.

The smallpox outbreak of 1837 claimed nearly 50 percent of the Arikara residents and 60 percent of their Hidatsa neighbors. The losses for the Mandan were even worse. Historians estimate that up to 95 percent of the mighty trading nation died in a matter of days. At Fort Union, the steamboat's next stop, the Assiniboine fell ill too. The disease spread across the region as people fled.

It was the end of an era. The mighty tribal trading network would never be the same. While the survivors concentrated on rebuilding, a power vacuum opened among the Great Plains tribes. The Sioux and Chippewa would have been logical choices to fill that void. But there was a new player on the scene—the United States government—and it was changing the rules of the game.

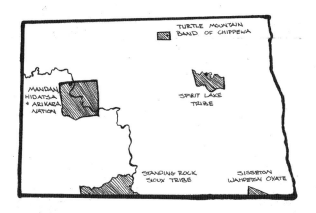

North Dakota reservations. *JoRelle Grover and Joseph Steinmann.*

RESERVATIONS AND THE RAILROAD

The U.S. government had plans for the land that would become North Dakota. The government asked tribal leaders to concentrate their villages, camps and hunting grounds in specific areas, to permit the building of frontier forts, roads and railways and to allow safe passage for white settlers. In exchange, the government promised the tribes annuities and use of designated lands. The treaties pushed the tribes away from development zones in the eastern part of the region and eventually onto Indian reservations, which increased the land available for white settlement.

Indian agents arrived on the scene to enforce the treaties. "He embodied a new character of white men unlike the previous trader, trappers and military men who had come up the Missouri," explained Carolyn Gilman and Mary Jane Schneider in *The Way to Independence: Memories of a Hidatsa Indian Family, 1840–1920.* "He did not come to blend into the native culture and society but to transform it. The agent intended to impose rules and regulations on the tribes and there was little the native people could do since he controlled the flow of trade goods on which the Missouri people had found themselves dependent."

On March 2, 1861, the land that would eventually become North Dakota first became the Dakota Territory. The Homestead Act of 1862 offered 160 acres of free, recently vacated land to settlers who stayed on the property for five years and paid a small filing fee. Homesteaders from the eastern United States and Europe arrived in the region, and competition for already limited resources increased.

Most of the frontier military forts in the Dakota Territory were built to support a series of United States Army missions to curb Native American resistance to the government's new systems and to protect railroad routes and clear the way for white settlements. Simmering tensions boiled over. Soldiers, tribal leaders and warriors, as well as Native American elders, women and children, lost their lives on five Civil War–era battlefields on North Dakota soil.

Tribes in the region were forced onto reservations under the watchful eyes of soldiers and Indian agents. Those who would not comply were pushed to the west and south, away from key development zones.

In 1864, President Lincoln signed a bill that allowed the Northern Pacific Railroad Company to develop and sell more than 50 million acres of land from Minnesota to Washington in exchange for developing a northern railroad route. The railroad would plot cities and recruit settlers and businesses to fill them.

The first economic and beer boom would occur before North Dakota even became a state. It all started the day the Northern Pacific tracks crossed the Red River and into Dakota Territory.

Chapter 2

SALOONS, SETTLEMENT AND STATEHOOD

The First Big Beer Boom, 1872-1889

The beer was cheap, the fiddling sharp, and the dancing sweaty.
—*Caleb Crain*, Necessary Errors

The first North Dakota beer boom started the moment the Northern Pacific Railroad tracks crossed the Minnesota state line and into the former tent city of Centralia on June 6, 1872. The scrappy little town was renamed Fargo to honor railroad investor (and Wells Fargo founder) William Fargo. The railroad's marketing campaigns in U.S., European and Scandinavian newspapers billed the Dakota Territory as an agricultural paradise, and the number of white settlers increased.

Early homesteaders in the territory were awarded land in the Red River Valley, along what would become the state's eastern border. The soil was rich from thousands of years as a glacial lake bottom, and early crop yields were promising. Word spread.

New waves of immigrants boarded trains operated by the same railroad that recruited them, and they went as far west as the rails could take them. The trickle of settlers became a flood, with thousands arriving every month. In 1870, there were just 2,405 people on the land that would become North Dakota. There would be 190,983 by 1890.

Some of the very first businesses to appear were saloons that served the workers who built the railroads and worked in the farm fields. Local breweries would soon follow. In just seventeen short years, the region would welcome sixteen commercial breweries and a staggering number of saloons. North Dakota's love affair with beer had officially begun.

Beer and Saloon Culture

Saloons were a gathering place for men in Dakota Territory. Women and children could stop by to fill up a bucket, pitcher, jar or jug with beer for family meals, but the activities inside were strictly male-oriented. Early saloons doubled as living rooms, kitchens and social centers for men who were living in tents, dugout sod houses, hotels and makeshift boardinghouses.

Saloons and taverns were originally housed in tents but moved into flat-front buildings and hotel lobbies as the cities developed. The working-class bars that served the railroad men and farm laborers were typically located near rivers and along railroad tracks. Typically, the deeper you went into town, the more upscale the establishments became.

Tavern owners made it easy to spend lots of time at the bar. They offered newspapers, job advice, gambling and poker games, free drinks and very cheap or complimentary lunches subsidized by the big Milwaukee and St. Louis breweries that supplied the beer before Dakota Territory started brewing its own. It was polite to treat buddies, business associates and even strangers to a free drink. It was considered rude to refuse and unthinkable not to return the favor. Smart bartenders and saloon owners would buy the first round to ensure that everybody felt obligated to return the favor and

The Brass Rail Saloon in Page was a typical nineteenth-century bar. *Alicia Underlee Nelson.*

buy more. It was almost impossible to plunk down a nickel for an eight-ounce glass of beer, drink it and head home.

Saloons were open twenty-four hours a day, seven days a week. This often wasn't technically legal, but it was lucrative, especially during the busiest seasons. The number of revelers swelled between August and October (when transient farmhands who worked on the territory's massive bonanza farms came into town to spend their harvest money), as well as whenever railroad employees came to the cities to get paid. These short-term residents and seasonal workers were a double-edged sword for the young cities.

On one hand, their labor was vital. The workers built the territory's transportation infrastructure and established agriculture as its primary industry. The saloons and taverns that served (and often overserved) them contributed thousands of dollars in licensing fees to city coffers. Fees for violations like selling beer after hours were affordable for bar owners, so they violated them cheerfully and often, preferring to spend a little money in fines rather than losing a lot of money by actually following the law. The city fathers looked the other way since the additional fees provided their towns with a steady stream of income.

But the alcohol-related shenanigans became harder to ignore. Early newspapers published stories of bar brawls, muggings, men passing out (and sometimes dying) in the streets following a bender and illegal gambling raids. There was even the occasional alcohol-fueled murder.

The Northern Pacific line pushed west toward the Missouri River, moving through Bismarck and Mandan in 1879. Bismarck would become the capital of the territory in 1883. In just a few years, these sister cities went from rough, frontier outposts with muddy streets to fully functioning cities with enough saloons to specialize. Charles Roby's saloon (located on today's 200 block of East Main Street in Mandan) was a popular gathering place, while Curley Sublette's Main Street Saloon was the watering hole of choice for older gents and cowboys just down the street.

There was room in the beer market for peddling entrepreneurs, too. Alex McKenzie would later become a political strongman, a champion of big business and one of North Dakota's most colorful and corrupt personalities. But in 1875, he was a young man on the rise, expanding his soft drink business to include his speciality, "Crrouc Beer." He peddled it through the streets of Bismarck in a wheelbarrow.

While the Northern Pacific Railroad moved west into Montana, crews laid track for the St. Paul, Minneapolis and Manitoba (SPM&M) Railway in

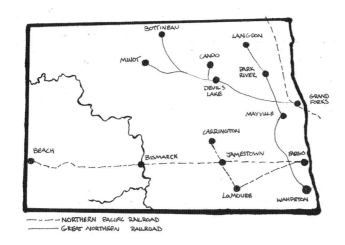

Railroads in the Dakota Territory by 1886. *JoRelle Grover and Joseph Steinmann.*

Fargo, which was later renamed the Great Northern Railway in 1889. The railroad had entered Grand Forks by 1881 and continued west to Devils Lake. The SPM&M reached a quiet spot near the Souris River in western Dakota Territory in 1886. This was Minot, nicknamed the "Magic City" because an entire tent city sprang up overnight around what was then the end of the line.

"It was a wild, roaring town in those days," according to a report by Colonel Clement Lounsberry. "There were 23 saloons, sporting houses, dance halls, gambling of every class, and a floating population of fully 2,500 during its very first year of its existence."

RED-LIGHT DISTRICTS

The sporting houses Colonel Lounsberry mentioned had nothing to do with sports. They were brothels overseen by enterprising madams, who often owned the homes and female boardinghouses where they based their operations.

Some of the courtesans who followed the railroad to serve the traveling salesmen, railroad crews and farmworkers operated independently on streets and in area parks. But by the 1880s, most prostitutes worked in established red-light districts. One of the most notorious was called The Hollow.

There were a few discreet prostitutes operating in Grand Forks, but the majority of sex workers in the sister cities of Grand Forks and East Grand

Forks were on the Minnesota side of the border. The Hollow in East Grand Forks was located near where the Red Lake and Red Rivers meet, near present-day Fourth Avenue and between the Division Avenue Bridge and Point Bridge. (The Point Bridge was later replaced by the Washington Street Bridge, which is two blocks east of The Hollow.) Prostitutes weren't allowed to move freely outside the red-light district, but the neighborhood itself wasn't exactly hidden. It sat just at the foot of the bridges that connected businesses in the two cities. Kids walked right past it on their way to school.

Fargo's red-light district was located north of First Avenue North between Second and Third Streets North. This neighborhood got a rough reputation back in 1871. Back then it was called Fargo in the Timber, named for its location along the shady banks of the Red River. The well-heeled residents of Fargo on the Prairie (near what's now Broadway and Main Avenue) took issue with the squatters, saloons and brothels near the river. They called the soldiers in from Fort Abercrombie to break up the party, pointing out that it was illegal for residents to sell alcohol on Sioux land. Two Fargo in the Timber residents were lawyers with friends in high places. These friends contacted the U.S. attorney general, who had no qualms with white residents living or selling alcohol on tribal land once a treaty was finalized. (He did ask them to stop cutting down the trees, though.) The Wahpeton and Sisseton Sioux ceded the land in 1873, and selling alcohol became officially legal in Fargo.

The lobby of Fargo's new city hall sits right on top of the site of one of The Hollow's most well-known brothels, the Crystal Palace. It was operated by Melvina Massey, easily the most successful African American businessperson in the city. It's a fitting tribute to an industry that paid regular fines as a makeshift licensing system. The brothels enjoyed additional police protection, and the city appreciated a steady revenue stream.

Prostitutes sometimes served beer to patrons in the brothels (we know because madams occasionally got busted for it), but they also drank and worked in establishments across the city. Citizens saw their elaborate hats peeking out of carriage windows as they went to work in three theaters and more than forty saloons and beer gardens. Some women worked out of the Coliseum, which offered vaudeville shows, a saloon and a particular brand of female companionship. Waitresses served balcony booths that had curtains in the front for privacy and discreet rear doors in case a patron had to make a quick exit. It's pretty clear that the action on stage wasn't the only attraction. The beer in their glasses might have been from a local brewery.

H. BOSE BREWERY (BISMARCK), 1873–?

Steamboat traffic along the Missouri River made Bismarck an attractive spot for the first commercial brewers in Dakota Territory. A series of advertisements in the *Bismarck Tribune* in July and August 1873 announced that H. Bose would supply lager beer to dealers at Fort Lincoln and Fort Rice.

This is the earliest recorded mention of lager brewed in the Dakota Territory. A lager is a bottom-fermented beer that's brewed and stored at a cool temperature for a period of weeks or months until it mellows and matures. (The word *lager* in German actually means "to warehouse" or "to store.") The cold slows down the yeast activity and limits the fruity notes that fermentation produces, giving lagers a cleaner, crisper taste than ale. Lagers are often pale in color, ranging from straw colored to a light amber. It was new to the territory but right on track with the beer trends of the day. Lagers would remain America's beer of choice for more than one hundred years.

H. Bose's lager didn't exactly take Bismarck-Mandan by storm. In April 1874, the same newspaper indicated that the brewery had "long since failed."

GIRARD & COMPANY (BISMARCK), 1874–1876

A new brewery would soon offer more compelling local beer. R.H. Girard (alternatively spelled Gerard), Carl Greve and a brewer we know only by his last name, Adams, built Girard & Company during the spring and summer of 1874. It was located on a ridge above the Missouri River, about one hundred feet north of where the east side of the Liberty Memorial Bridge stands today.

The group brewed lager beer in a cluster of wood-frame buildings along the river. The brewery contained a malt kiln, an icehouse and a cold storage cellar. The staff almost certainly used blocks of ice from the nearby river to cool and store lager.

The owners also took advantage of the brewery's picturesque location and opened a beer garden nearby. It had arbors for shade and views of the Missouri River.

Kalberer & Walter (Bismarck), 1876–1883

Jacob Kalberer and August Walter bought the Girard & Company brewery in 1876 and renamed it Kalberer & Walter. (They weren't super creative with brewery names back then, apparently.) An advertisement in the *Bismarck Tribune* on July 18, 1877, stated that the duo produced "ale and beer," which likely meant ale and lager, since the brewery had ample cold storage space, an icehouse and a riverside location.

The brewery sold keg beer to local saloons and began bottling on site in 1880. The Kalberer & Walter brewery was operated by its owners and leased to other brewers until it was destroyed by fire in 1883.

Star Brewery (Bismarck), 1876–1882

The Star Brewery gave Kalberer and Walter a little competition when it opened on Third Street on Bismarck's south side in 1876. It was owned by Judson E. Walker, who also owned and operated the St. Louis Liquor Store, a large liquor wholesaler on the south side of town. He likely operated the brewery in partnership with John D. Wakeman until 1880, when it was run by brewmaster John Fisher and businessman Chris Yengen.

The Star Brewery offered the most comprehensive North Dakota beer lineup to date, including lager, ale, porter and stout. The beer Walker brewed was probably influenced by what sold well in his store.

The Star Brewery operated until June 1882, around the time that Bismarck's economic bubble burst. The overmortgaged Walker sold the property to Charles R. Williams, a Bismarck saloon owner, who used the building to store beer arriving via railcar from Milwaukee. The Star Brewery was destroyed by fire just a few weeks later, on August 4, 1882. Williams would continue to store, distribute and bottle beer in quart- and pint-sized bottles for Franz Falk Brewing Company and Phillip Best Brewing Company (which would later become Pabst).

Milwaukee Brewery (Bismarck), 1884–1889

Both of Bismarck's brewery buildings had burned by the time the Milwaukee Brewery opened in 1884. It was owned and operated by Frederick (Fred)

Miller. Yes, *that* Fred Miller, *the* Fred Miller—the man whose empire gave us Miller Lite, Miller Genuine Draft (MGD) and Miller High Life—was a Bismarck business owner.

Miller was German, born Friedrich Eduard Johannes Müller in 1824. He learned how to brew at Sigmaringen, in what is now southern Germany; immigrated to the United States in 1854; settled in Wisconsin; and established the Frederick Miller Brewing Company in Milwaukee in 1855. Miller planned to distribute beer brewed at the satellite location in Bismarck by Missouri River steamboat (the brewery stood on a bluff overlooking the docks) and eventually by rail.

This was an unusual move. Other breweries at the time simply shipped their product using the new refrigerated railcars that were revolutionizing the beer industry. But Miller and his investors, which included brewmaster, construction foreman and brewery superintendent George Eckhardt and manager John Legler, had big production goals and wanted to get their beer deeper into Montana ahead of the competition.

Milwaukee Brewing Company beer was sold in kegs and bottles in the territory and as far as the rails would carry it. It produced enough beer to

Milwaukee Brewery in Bismarck. *State Historical Society of North Dakota (SHSND), 00738-002.*

make the Milwaukee Brewery one of the top two production breweries in what would become North Dakota.

Miller's sons—Fred, Emil and Ernst—needed a year of hands-on brewing experience to get into a prestigious brewing program in New York. They learned on the job in Bismarck, drinking beer and catching glimpses of Sioux Chief Sitting Bull, who was camped with his people near the brewery. The brewery was planning a westward expansion in 1887 when Fred Miller took ill. When he died in 1888, his eldest son Ernst G. Miller's corporation took over operations. The brewery's biggest challenge lay just ahead.

FORT PEMBINA (PEMBINA), 1874–?

Residents in another Dakota Territory steamboat town were also enjoying locally brewed beer as early as the 1870s. Sutler A.W. Stiles is credited with running a brewery on the grounds of Fort Pembina from 1874 to 1875. Since the fort was occupied until 1895, it's likely that the brewery operated during at least some of those years as well.

NATHAN MYRICK'S STORE (PEMBINA), 1875–?

There was a second brewery in town during the same decade. Edward L. Drewry ran a brewery operation in Nathan Myrick's store in Pembina in the 1870s. Drewy attended school in Minnesota and worked in St. Paul before moving to Pembina in 1874. He was also, it seems, a pretty talented conversationalist.

"We often went to see Drewry, not because he ran a brewery, but because we liked to visit Drewy—liked to talk with him," said Pembina journalist and historian Charles Lee in *A History of Pembina County*. "Perhaps we visited him too often, talked with him too much, he got discouraged, pulled up, left the country and went to Winnipeg."

Drewry did indeed go north to Winnipeg. He opened the Redwood Brewery there in 1877 and became an esteemed member of Manitoba society.

Pembina Brewing Company (Pembina), 1882–1889

The Pembina Brewing Company was built in the forest south of the Pembina River in 1882. It opened for business in 1884, when C. Thomas of Winnipeg and a brewer known to us only as Mumberg started producing porter, ale and lager.

The Pembina Brewing Company changed ownership several times. It was probably staffed and owned by people from nearby Manitoba. It served the local population until 1889 and saw several larger distribution breweries open to the south, along the Red River.

Fargo Lager Beer Brewery (Fargo), 1879

In 1879, Joseph Prokosch built the Fargo Lager Beer Brewery at Second Street North near Fourth Avenue, in the eastern corner of downtown Fargo. It was located just west of the Red River near the railroad tracks. Prokosch sold the brewery to a Norwegian immigrant named Ole Aslesen in 1880.

Fargo Brewery (Fargo), 1880–1889

Ole Aslesen immigrated to the United States as a child, living in Minnesota and Iowa before coming to Fargo and purchasing Prokosch's brewery. He called his new business the Fargo Brewery. An established saloonkeeper named Charles Hult became a co-owner and operating partner in 1881.

Together they produced at least five thousand barrels of beer a year. Newspaper reports indicate that the brewery had the capacity to produce six to seven thousand barrels a year, but it's unclear if they were able to maximize production. Fargo Brewery lager was sold throughout the city (including in saloons like Hult's) and was distributed within a one-hundred-mile radius of Fargo by rail.

The 1884 Sanborn Fire Insurance Map gives us a basic layout of the Fargo Brewery. The brick building included an on-site malt house, several rooms for brewing and large cold storage cellars that could accommodate the 1,200 tons of ice the brewery needed every year.

Coal-fired steam was used to power the brewing operations, wood fires heated the mash and candles illuminated the brewhouse. Fire was a constant threat to this and other breweries of the era. Many, like the breweries operated by Aslesen's contemporaries in Bismarck, burned before volunteer fire departments could arrive with wet blankets and buckets.

RED RIVER VALLEY BREWERY (FARGO), 1881–1889

The Red River Valley Brewery (also known as Red River Brewing Company) shook up the Fargo brewing scene in 1881. John G. Kraenzlein built the two-story brick structure just a few feet away from his rivals at the Fargo Brewery. Kraenzlein was a veteran brewer who had overseen operations at a Minneapolis brewery and supervised a malt house in Milwaukee, so he got right to work. Fargo beer fans had Red River Valley Brewery beer in their glasses by December 1881.

L. Rueping, J.A. (Adam) Klinkert and J.G.F. Schneidler took over on January 17, 1883. Klinkert, a German immigrant, had been brewing for Kraenzlein since July 1882.

The Red River Valley Brewery sold lager and a wiener beer that was a very popular table beer for families in the territory. (Yes, that's right, wiener beer. The good people of the Red River Valley would walk right up and order a wiener. Take a moment to let that sink in.)

Now that we've all stopped giggling like twelve-year-olds, we should probably talk about what this wiener beer (sometimes spelled "weiner") actually was. It's probably a corruption of the word *Vienner*, which was how brewers and customers identified a lager made in Vienna. The "er" suffix is a common way to note where a beer style originated—a pilsner is from Pilsen, a Berliner weisse is from Berlin and so on. A Vienna lager is a medium-bodied, amber-colored beer that was a common, low-alcohol table beer in Mexico and in the United States before Prohibition. Klinkert's wiener beer probably tasted like a modern Schell's Firebrick or a Dos Equis Amber. The Red River Valley Brewery was shipping 1,920 quart bottles of wiener beer daily by 1888.

The brewery challenged the Milwaukee Brewery in Bismarck for the title of the largest brewery in the territory. A January 18, 1884 article in the *Moorhead Weekly News* reported that the Red River Valley Brewery's capacity was eighteen thousand barrels per year and that its beer was sold "north as far as Winnipeg, on both the Dakota and Minnesota sides of the Red river [*sic*]; south on all road as far as they extend; west to Bismarck; east halfway to St. Paul." Later estimates indicated that the

Red River Valley Brewing Company label. *Forum Communications Company Collection, Historical and Cultural Society of Clay County (HCSCC).*

brewery may have approached twenty to twenty-five thousand barrels per year.

The Red River Valley Brewery contained nineteen thirty-five-barrel tubs, rooms for storing and filling kegs and two large beer cellars. An icehouse on the brewery grounds held the four thousand tons of ice per year needed to make its beer.

The brewery probably grew hops on the premises. Wild hops were spotted at the brewery site before it was excavated to create permanent flood protection in 2016.

A staff of twenty experienced malters also malted barley on the brewery grounds. The Milwaukee Brewery had tried to do the same in Bismarck, but Fargo's location in the heart of farm country meant the Red River Valley Brewery could source barley from local farmers on both sides of the river. An 1888 article in the *Leading Industries of the West* reported that the brewery took in fifty-five thousand bushels of barley from local farmers that year, contributing $36,000 to the local farm economy.

The brewery had two malt rooms that could accommodate thirty thousand bushels of malt and soak tubs that could hold five hundred bushels of barley at a time. A bushel is a unit of measurement that contains sixty-four pints of dry goods. Since this can be a little tricky to visualize, it might help to imagine an old-fashioned, eighteen- by twelve-inch wooden bushel basket.

The barley that farmers grew during this era would have been very different from the barley North Dakota farmers grow today. "Those varieties would have been very tall and very weak," said Dr. Richard

Horsley, professor, department head and barley breeder for North Dakota State University's Department of Plant Sciences in Fargo. "They probably had less nitrogen fertilizer, so it would have been a struggle to keep them standing. The yield was much lower than now." Less barley per bushel for the farmer meant less malt for the brewer, so Dakota Territory brewers would have needed to procure more barley per batch than modern brewers to create a comparable beer.

The steamboat crews called the strip of land by the SPM&M tracks "Brewery Point" because both Fargo breweries were visible right across the river from a competitor in Moorhead, Minnesota. The three breweries shared suppliers and a beer-loving customer base.

LARKIN BROTHERS BREWERY (MOORHEAD, MINNESOTA), 1875

Moorhead's first brewery was built by Canadian brothers Joseph and George Larkin in 1875. They constructed a fifty-six- by twenty-four-foot building near the current site of Moorhead's Riverfront Park tennis courts. Their brewing equipment arrived on the steamboat from Winnipeg, and the pair took orders for ale that spring and summer. They wouldn't fill many of them. Ale has a shorter shelf life than lager, which limited the Larkin brothers' distribution area and may have been responsible for the quality issues that newspaper reports hinted at.

Drinkers in the region had already demonstrated a fondness for lager, which the Larkins probably never even had a chance to make, since they arrived in town when the ice necessary for lager production was already off the river. The business was in foreclosure within the year. John Erickson, a Swedish immigrant who owned a saloon, two hotels and several other businesses, took over the brewery in 1876.

ERICKSON'S BREWERY (MOORHEAD, MINNESOTA), 1876–1895

John Erickson brought the brewery's production to 1,835 barrels in 1881. His brewhouse could produce up to four thousand barrels of beer annually.

The lager brewed there was sold in saloons and hotels in Moorhead and Fargo (including those owned by Erickson himself) and throughout the region on the SPM&M Railroad and Northern Pacific lines. He ruffled a few feathers when he shipped his beer east to the proud beer city of St. Paul, a bold move for a fledgling brewery.

Many of the brewery's ingredients were locally sourced. Between six and a dozen seasonal workers malted barley that Erickson purchased from farmers in the region in the on-site malt house. Pigs feasted on the spent grain in a nearby pig yard. Erickson also planted three acres of hops near the brewery in 1883.

Erickson's head brewer was a German immigrant named Fred (but also called Fritz) Wachsmuth. The pair worked together until Wachsmuth was fired in May 1884. That decision resulted in tragedy. After battling a blaze as a member of the local fire department, Wachsmuth had a few drinks and returned to the brewery, which, until that fateful day, was also the home he had shared with his wife and baby. His friends were outside, loading up the family's belongings, when they heard a shot ring out. They ran to the brewery's pig yard to find that Wachsmuth had taken his own life. He was thirty-five. The packed church at Wachsmuth's funeral and his burial at Prairie Home Cemetery in Moorhead are a testament to his standing in the community.

Brewer Joseph Jennister replaced Wachsmuth, but by then, Erickson was struggling to pay his many mortgages. The brewery was sold at sheriff's sales at least twice before the First National Bank of Moorhead foreclosed on the property in 1895. Erickson's business failures didn't seem to harm his reputation, though. He served as Moorhead's mayor three times.

The two breweries in Fargo had lost a competitor just across the Minnesota border but would gain more within the territory. Modest Jamestown, founded in 1872 in the southeast part of Dakota Territory, didn't evolve into a major retail center like Fargo or a political player like Bismarck. But it held its own in the 1880s brewing scene.

South Side Brewery (Jamestown), 1880–1889

The first brewery in town was called a variety of names, including the Jamestown Brewery, the City Brewery, Henry Danner's Brewery and the South Side Brewery. It was owned and operated by Henry Danner,

Hops. *PhotoRx*.

a professionally trained brewer from Jefferson, Wisconsin.

He built a thirty- by sixty-foot brick brewery on his property along the James River, east of Klaus Park, in 1880. The newspaper said it was the largest building in town. By 1882, the South Side Brewery was producing fifteen barrels of lager a day (which had increased to thirty barrels a day by 1886), and Danner claimed to sell two hundred kegs a week in and around Jamestown.

That sounds like a lot for a small town (Jamestown had about one thousand residents in 1883), but the little city anchored a strong beer scene. There were twenty-three saloons in town, as well as a large German-speaking population south of the city that had a strong cultural appreciation for beer. Danner also shipped beer to cities along the Northern Pacific line. The tracks ran right by his brewery.

Danner added a steam engine to power brewing operations and built an on-site malt house. It's also possible that Danner used local hops in his beer, since modern homebrewers report spotting wild hops near the brewery site in Klaus Park.

Danner sold the brewery to Phillip Bauer in 1886. Bauer lived in Iowa, so his son, Otto, oversaw operations in Jamestown. The brewery was heavily damaged by a fire in 1887. It was rebuilt just before statehood brought unexpected changes to the beer industry.

JAMESTOWN BREWING COMPANY (JAMESTOWN), 1885–1889

Jamestown's second brewery opened in 1885. It was called Jamestown Brewing Company, although the locals also called it the North Side Brewery since it was located along a loop in the James River near Fourth Avenue North. Jamestown Brewing Company was a family business all the way around.

The original wooden brewery building was built by Oswald Kulewatz, who was in the bottling business with his brother, Frederick. They partnered with another pair of brothers of German descent named Otto and Gaudenz

Gasal. Oswald Kulewatz served as brewmaster, and his beer was sold in Jamestown's saloons and distributed by rail around the region.

The trio enlarged the building and added a new bottling works in 1885, just before the brewery had a run of bad luck in 1886. It was destroyed by a fire in February, and the rebuilt structure was damaged by a freakishly early April tornado just weeks later. Kulewatz was brewing beer again by May 1 but would resign by September. The plucky Gasal brothers pressed on. They were working in a brand-new brick brewery by the end of that unlucky year. Both Jamestown breweries would continue brewing until statehood brought them more bad luck.

Dobmeier Brewery (Grand Forks), 1881–1898

While German brewers got established in Jamestown, another German immigrant was already hard at work in his brewhouse in Grand Forks. Jacob Dobmeier opened the Dobmeier Brewery south of Grand Forks' fledgling business district in what is now Central Park in 1882. He started the brewery with business and brewing partners Jacob Gahr and Phillip Metzler in 1881 but bought them out a few months later.

He added on to the building in 1883, just in time to celebrate his marriage to Elizabeth Dastert on November 29, 1884, with a spectacular party at the brewery. Local saloon and hotel owners, along with a cadet band, marched in a procession from Byrne's Office Saloon and up Third Street to find the groom.

It was a big crowd. Grand Forks had twenty-six bars by 1885, and more than half of them (fifteen total) were on Third Street. Dobmeier led his guests to the brewery for "free flowing beer" and on to a banquet hall, where a feast of fifty turkeys, sauerkraut, oysters and towering cakes awaited them. Dobmeier led the crowd in "Auld Lang Syne" and a few German tunes, and everybody danced Irish jigs until midnight.

Dobmeier worked as hard as he played. He was the sole owner of the business but later brought brewers Jacob Gahr and Phillip Metzler on board to help. He added a malt house in 1886. The Dobmeier Brewery produced twelve thousand barrels of beer in 1886, just under the brewery's capacity of fourteen thousand barrels a year, making it the third-largest brewery in the territory.

An advertisement in the September 12, 1888 edition of the *Grand Forks Daily Herald* reveals that the brewery produced "MUMM, Bavarian and

Bohemian export beer." Dobmeier's MUMM beer was a low alcohol "near beer" that he continued to brew and sell during a long period of prohibition. His Bohemian export beer was likely a malty-sweet, medium-bodied, Bohemian-style pilsner that was consistent with popular styles brewed elsewhere in the region at the time. If the opinion of the author of a *Grand Forks Daily Herald* account on December 19, 1886, represented the views of the drinking public, Dobmeier's "matchless Bavarian beer," which "drives the German soul to ecstasies," was probably a pretty big seller as well.

There were two other breweries serving local customers in Dakota Territory in the years before statehood. They were both established in small towns, and at one point, they were both operated by the same man.

WAHPETON BREWERY (WAHPETON), 1882–1888

German immigrant Carl Stofft founded the Wahpeton Brewery in the Red River Valley town of the same name in 1882. The small town south of Fort Abercrombie had just four hundred residents in the 1880 census. Stofft worked with a local contractor named Hoppe to build a small wood-frame building on the west bank of the river one block north of the bridge that still connects Wahpeton with its sister city, Breckenridge, Minnesota.

The brewery, which was owned by several people during its existence, did a brisk business with local customers in surrounding counties, including newly arrived German-speaking settlers and Bohemian immigrants from what is now the Czech Republic. These groups would be important beer consumers for brewers, past and present.

Bohemian groups also settled near Pisek, Conway and Lankin in the northeast and Dickinson and Montrail County farther west. The Germans and the Germans from Russia (who had lived in tightknit communities near the Black Sea in what is now Ukraine) settled in a wide band across what would become the lower part of the state, between Wahpeton and Bismarck. They were opposed to the temperance movement, which was gaining momentum in the East. The final Wahpeton Brewery owner, Michael Schmitt, thought that temperance sympathizers were behind the fire that destroyed his brewery in October 1888.

TURTLE MOUNTAIN BREWERY (DUNSEITH), 1887–1889

While the Wahpeton Brewery burned, Carl Stofft was busy brewing farther north in Dunseith, a tiny city in Rolette County, just south of the Canadian border on the SPM&M (later the Great Northern) line and right next to the Turtle Mountain Chippewa reservation in Belcourt. Stofft built Turtle Mountain Brewery in 1887, when the town had a population of just 150 people. He enlisted the help of a local cooper named Francis Higgins to make what the *Turtle Mountain Star* called "custom vats" for the brewing system and stayed on as the head brewer.

Turtle Mountain Brewery's address was in Dunseith, but it was actually rural, located in a spot that likely used water from a nearby spring. A retrospective article in the June 16, 1932 edition of the *Turtle Mountain Star* recalled that the brewery was built into the side of a hill at the foot of the Turtle Mountains about one mile outside the city, and "many were the parties staged in the willow grove nearby." The setting sounds both beautiful and bacchanalian.

As the railroads moved west through Dakota Territory in the 1880s, they ran smack dab into another boom. Cowboys from the Black Hills in what is now South Dakota, as well as Colorado and Wyoming were moving their herds north to the Little Missouri River Valley and the starkly beautiful badlands near Medora and Dickinson. The cowboys worked long days and moved with the herd. And where there were cowboys, you'd also find alcohol and women.

DANCE HALL ANTICS

C.O. Armstrong, a rancher who homesteaded near Fairfield, northeast of Medora, had some pretty wild stories about how the cowboys partied with dance hall girls in the prairie town of Winona in Emmons County, deep in the heart of Germans-from-Russia country. Winona is a ghost town now, but it was founded as Devil's Colony in 1874. The name fit.

Devil's Colony was created to serve the soldiers at Fort Yates, who monitored the nearby Standing Rock Sioux reservation. Since alcohol was forbidden on reservation land, the soldiers made the town their playground, drinking, gambling and dancing all night long with both

The Wabek Saloon looks like a typical frontier watering hole. *Jack Dura.*

saloon girls and women from the reservation. Farmers and ranchers soon joined them.

In 1876, additional troops arrived at Fort Yates to force the last of the Sioux resistors onto the reservation after allied Native American forces defeated General Custer at the Battle of the Greasy Grass, also known as Custer's Last Stand. When Chief Sitting Bull finally surrendered at Fort Buford in western Dakota Territory in 1881, he wanted it noted that he was the last of his tribe to give in to the reservation system.

There was a lot of tension and testosterone in this little prairie village of just over one hundred permanent residents. It didn't help that almost everybody had a weapon. The parties could—and often did—get dangerous.

"There were two fiddlers playing for the dance; the window was up and the musicians were sitting by the window," C.O. Armstrong told a Works Progress Administration (WPA) interviewer. "All of the girls had on cowpunchers' hats. In those days they danced the old fashioned way, dancing one way and then reversing, and the cowpunchers would shoot every time they would reverse, and they weren't very particular where they shot. The fiddlers were getting rather scared, so they dropped their fiddles and went out the window. We had some pretty good fiddlers in the bunch, so two of the cowboys picked up the fiddles and started to play, and the dance went on."

In addition to shooting up the dance floor, these cowboys also had the dance hall girls line up so they could shoot glasses out of their hands. Being a saloon girl or a dance hall girl was never a particularly safe occupation (customers fought for their attention, tempers flared and many girls had to forcibly convince customers that the majority of them were not, in fact, prostitutes, despite their makeup, dyed hair and scandalously short skirts), but this was extreme, even by Wild West standards. But at least nobody died that day. That wasn't always the case.

One saloon girl in Winona defended herself against an overzealous patron, hitting and killing him by smashing a spittoon on his head. Shooting in the air and the threat of gun violence were common, so saloon owners like Maggie Murphey packed heat so they could threaten their customers right back. When a saloon girl shot a man in her room above the bar, her boss helped her dispose of the body. We know they were drinking beer in at least one of Winona's nine saloons because the duo buried the body under empty beer kegs in the cellar. When the supplier came to claim the empties, the saloon owner told him the story. The vendor simply took the kegs and left. The secret (and presumably the body) stayed in Winona.

Winona's sheriff was a practical man. He realized that the men of the town weren't equipped to go toe to toe with a bunch of drunk, gun-toting transients. They were outnumbered and outgunned and just tried to weather the storm.

Beer Moves West

The beer in Winona was brought in overland from a railway stop in what is now South Dakota. But the fortune seekers riding the railroads west could get beer much more easily. They got off the train in western cities like Dickinson, where they downed a few nickel schooners of beer at saloons like the one in the Atkinson Hotel and started looking for work.

They might have been drinking beer from the Milwaukee Brewery in Bismarck. Miller's beer had already reached farther west to Medora, near what would be the Montana border, by 1884. The Marquis de Mores, a

French nobleman and friend to future president and onetime Dakota Territory rancher Teddy Roosevelt, had a meatpacking business there that would send the territory's beef east using the same refrigerated railcars that sent its beer west. The colorful bluffs that surround the city would become part of Theodore Roosevelt National Park, North Dakota's most visited attraction, in 1947. But these two famous Medora residents would be long gone by then.

The Dakota Territory cattle boom went bust during the harsh winter of 1886–87. Nearly 70 percent of cattle died. The big ranchers from outside the region cut their losses and moved out. Theodore Roosevelt and the Marquis de Mores were among them.

DANCES AND COMMUNITY CELEBRATIONS

The ranchers who stayed on bought up their land and livestock. Small towns in and around Medora and Wibaux, Montana, just thirty-five miles to the west, remained linked through social gatherings. Dances featuring the same fiddle music that was popular at the frontier forts and dance halls were especially well attended. Since ranches were typically twenty to twenty-five miles apart, no experienced rider thought that thirty-five miles on horseback was too far to travel for a good time. Newcomers didn't always fare as well.

B.F. "Doc" Spry, who ranched near Marmarth in Slope County, near the Montana border, told a WPA interviewer about a cowboy named Abe Owens who took a neighbor's visiting sister to a dance in Wibaux. The couple and a female chaperone made it to the party in a buggy just fine but ran into trouble when the object of the cowboy's affections decided to ride a horse on the way back.

When they stopped, the exhausted woman, who developed horrible saddle sores, dismounted and promptly fainted. The chaperone nursed her, and the gallant cowboy visited every neighbor he could think of so she could rest indoors. Their first date turned into a meandering, nine-day, three-hundred-mile journey. It must have worked, though, because she married him.

The folks in and around early Valley City, in the central part of what's now North Dakota, didn't have to travel as far for a good time. Farm families lived closer to one another than ranching families in western Dakota Territory did and were able to come into town for dances and community celebrations like the ones businessman, farmer and inventor Albert Hoiland described to

Very cold beer in Williston. *State Historical Society of North Dakota (SHSND), William E. (Bill) Shemorry Photograph Collection, 1-6-18-13.*

a WPA interviewer. "Dancing was the chief form of recreation," Hoiland said. "The people danced the folk dances, waltzes, schottisches, polkas, gallop ryewaltzes, and heel-and-toe and square dances."

They threw some great holiday parties too, like a Fourth of July picnic that Hoiland recalled. There were baseball games, races and two twenty-foot tables full of food for snacking throughout the day. The men all chipped in a dollar to pay for the supplies to make lemonade and buy several gallons of wine and eighteen eight-gallon kegs of beer that cost three dollars each. Then everyone hit the fifty- by fifty-foot dance floor, which was built up on a platform. "The crowd started dancing at sundown and kept it up until daylight," said Hoiland.

STATEHOOD

The party was raging 24/7 in Dakota Territory in the 1880s. The saloons, brothels and dance halls were packed; the brewers were busy; the beer was flowing; and men, women and children danced until dawn across the territory. But not everybody was happy about it.

A motley crew of women's suffrage advocates, temperance societies, clergymen, farm wives and Scandinavian immigrants had been steadily calling for a complete alcohol ban for years. Their efforts and a growing national movement against alcohol consumption persuaded the rural residents of 70 percent of the territory's counties to go dry after 1887. But since cities could (and did) opt out, brewing, drinking and dancing continued. But it wouldn't last.

In 1889, a very slim majority—just 1,159 souls—voted to abolish alcohol in the new state of North Dakota. When North Dakota entered the union on November 2, 1889, it did so as a dry state. The party was over—at least officially. Now if North Dakotans wanted a beer, they were going to have to find a clever way to get it. And that's exactly what they did.

Chapter 3

BLIND PIGS, JAG WAGONS AND BEER RUNNERS

Getting a Drink During Prohibition, 1890-1932

Prohibition proved that Americans were a nation of ingenious drinkers.
—Ryan Dearinger

When residents of the new state of North Dakota woke up on the morning of November 3, 1889, they probably asked themselves the same questions that have modern readers scratching their heads: What the heck happened? How had such a hard-partying state gone dry?

Saloon and brewery owners, politicians and city leaders didn't see the temperance movement as a threat until it had already landed its knockout punch. Even temperance leaders seemed conflicted about their victory. A celebratory parade in Jamestown was quietly canceled.

The temperance movement in North Dakota started with the Anglo-Saxon civic and business leaders who held power and influence in the East and the mainline Protestant and Catholic parishioners and clergy who were tired of their towns' wild reputations. These reformers wanted a strong, prosperous community made up of educated, reasonable citizens held together by strong nuclear families. They also exalted women as the keepers of the home and the guardians of morality and virtue.

This gave frontier women an opportunity to influence the debate. In the cities, influential society wives started to wear temperance ribbons and sign pledges saying they'd abstain from alcohol and asked their husbands and sons to do the same. They founded local branches of national organizations like the Woman's Christian Temperance Union (WCTU). The temperance movement was closely linked to women's suffrage, and powerful women in the Red River Valley worked to advance both causes.

Rural women took up the cause for both moral and practical reasons. Farm wives and daughters worked as hard as men but enjoyed few of the same rights and opportunities. If their husbands were out drinking, it was the wives who picked up the slack. If the men spent too much money treating friends at the bar, their female dependents had few ways to replace that income.

Many men supported temperance as well. Special interest groups like the Anti-Saloon League (ASL) and fraternal organizations like the International Order of Good Templars (IOGT) grew out of the temperance movement across the country. Teetotalers organized by county, which resulted in a targeted and effective grass-roots movement.

In North Dakota, beliefs about alcohol consumption were influenced by the cultural beliefs of the region's two largest immigrant groups, the Norwegians and the Germans. Some Norwegians thought that dancing and drinking were sinful and had been part of temperance movements in Norway. More secular Norwegians agreed with their urban Swedish, Danish and Anglo-Saxon neighbors that public drunkenness was a social problem and saloon owners held too much financial and political power. No matter their class or religious background, nearly every Norwegian could read, and many followed the temperance coverage in Norwegian newspapers.

The Germans, both from the Rhineland and the Germans from Russia, felt differently. German speakers arrived in the territory later than their Scandinavian counterparts and were still getting established in the years just before statehood. They were less interested in broader civic engagement and more focused on farming and building tightknit communities like the ones they'd left in Russia, united by language and shared values. Those values (and those of their Czech neighbors) included a tradition of brewing and enjoying beer.

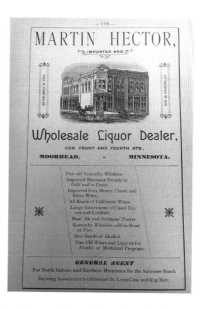

Businesses shipped beer into dry North Dakota by rail. *From the* 1891 Fargo and Moorhead Directory.

"Working hard led to celebrating—at wedding dances, sports events, harvest parties," Frank White, assistant professor of sociology at the University of North Dakota, told the *Bismarck Tribune* on December 9, 2012. "In the 'old country,' alcohol was part of life, and people didn't think of it as a negative in their culture."

Most German-speaking immigrants voted against prohibition, but it wasn't enough. It would be illegal to buy, sell or manufacture alcohol in North Dakota on July 1, 1890. That gave North Dakotans time to drink up or stock up.

THE BREWERIES REACT

The superintendent at the Milwaukee Brewery in Bismarck started dismantling the brewing equipment as soon as the election results were confirmed. It was shipped back to headquarters in Milwaukee, and brewery operations moved back east. The beer served at the brewery's last hurrah, an opulent 1889 New Year's Eve Ball that featured an extravagant meal and an orchestra, was probably shipped in from Milwaukee.

The mood was less festive at company headquarters. Prohibition would cost the brewery an estimated $200,000. The massive, seven-story building stood vacant until 1900, when it was sold to Issac P. Baker, who was, ironically, a teetotaler. He used it as a storage facility and seed house.

In Grand Forks, Jacob Dobmeier wasn't giving in quite so easily. He demanded that the new state government reimburse him exactly $72,640 for the losses Dobmeier Brewery would suffer under prohibition. The brewer had many important friends in North Dakota—seventy-two prominent business owners in Grand Forks signed his petition.

The legislators weren't impressed by the show of support. Negotiations continued until Senator John Haggart offered up the only compromise the lawmakers could agree on: $5,000 to every brewery in North Dakota. Dobmeier and his counterparts in Bismarck, Dunseith, Jamestown and Fargo had spent years building businesses that were about to become illegal. They needed every penny they could get.

The *Turtle Mountain Star* reported that the brewery in Dunseith served beer until statehood. It also reported that the city's four saloons kept operating well after prohibition was in effect, in open defiance of state law, so it's probable that the brewery's beer was still served in local bars until supplies ran out.

In Jamestown, absentee owner Phillip Bauer and his son and manager, Otto Bauer, had rebuilt their brewery after a fire in 1887. The $5,000 reimbursement from the state wasn't enough to help the South Side Brewery transform into a new business. Ownership of the property reverted to original owner and brewmaster Henry Danner, who later sold the building, which was demolished in 1900. The Gasal brothers had similar problems across town. Their North Side Brewery, which had been painstakingly rebuilt after both a fire and a tornado, stood vacant until it was torn down in 1904.

Louis Rueping and John A. Klinkert from the Red River Valley Brewery stayed in the beer business and gave the Miller brothers a little friendly competition in their home state. They opened Klinkert Brewing Company in Superior, Wisconsin, in 1890. They used malt produced in the Fargo facility. Klinkert left the partnership in 1898, and the brewery later become the Northern Brewing Company. For a time, it was Superior's leading beer supplier and operated until 1967.

Ole Aslesen of the Fargo Brewery also took his brewing talents elsewhere, but he didn't need to go nearly as far to do it. He operated Aslesen & Blegen saloon in Moorhead from 1891 to 1899. And he got back into the brewing business in 1897, when he bought the vacant Erickson Brewery in Moorhead and recruited Joseph Jennister (the brewmaster who took over after Fred Wachmuth's death) as the head brewer. Asleson ran the brewery with his son until a devastating fire in 1901 caused $10,000 in damage. His insurance only covered $3,000. Aslesen cut his losses and retired from the brewing business.

Dobmeier Brewery in Grand Forks was the only pre-statehood brewery still in business on North Dakota soil after 1890. It operated as a malt house and also continued to produce MUMM, Dobmeier's low-alcohol near beer, since beer with less than 2 percent alcohol by volume (ABV) was technically allowed under prohibition laws.

Dobmeier's low-alcohol temperance beer was legal, but other activities at the brewery were not. A police raid in 1898 revealed that Dobmeier was also brewing strong beer and supporting illegal gambling at the North Dakota location.

But the well-connected brewer had already supplemented his North Dakota brewery with one in East Grand Forks, Minnesota. His East Grand Forks Weiner Brewery opened in the summer of 1891. It specialized in the malty, amber-colored beer that had taken the Red River Valley by storm a few years earlier in Fargo. It would eventually produce eighteen thousand barrels of beer a year.

THE PARTY MOVES TO BORDER CITIES

Residents of Grand Forks had it easy during the Prohibition era. If people wanted a legal drink, they just went across the bridge that spanned the Red River and into a bustling party zone along DeMers Avenue.

Drinkers only had to go a few feet over the state line to grab a beer. By 1892, there were thirty-three saloons in East Grand Forks' bar district, twenty-two of them on the first block of DeMers Avenue alone. That number would swell to forty-six by 1903 and forty-eight by 1908. Tavern owners later distributed trade tokens to be redeemed for food and drinks to customers on both sides of the river.

Dobmeier's weiner beer was sold at many of the taverns of the day, which soon boasted updates like electric lights and bars made of quartered oak. The locals at the turn of the century were also drinking beer from Budweiser and Schlitz Brewing Company in Milwaukee; Minnesota favorites from Hamm's Brewing Company, Duluth Brewing and Malting Company and Minneapolis Brewing Company; and brews from G. Heileman Brewing Company in La Crosse, Wisconsin, and Gund Brewing Company in Cleveland, Ohio. Regional breweries operated eleven cold storage warehouses in East Grand Forks, including the Hamm's beer depot at 401 DeMers Avenue, which is now in the National Register of Historic Places.

Trade tokens provided by East Grand Forks saloons, courtesy of Charlotte Helgeson. *Alicia Underlee Nelson.*

North Dakota residents who didn't live near border cities could order beer from alcohol wholesalers. It was just as easy and legal as using a mail-order catalogue. Wholesalers shipped alcohol into North Dakota by rail until the 1913 Webb-Kenyon Act closed that legal loophole.

The same trains that carried beer out of eastern Minnesota cities also brought drinkers into the region. Saloon owners in Moorhead made it almost comically easy for residents and travelers in Fargo to cross the river for a drink by offering free rides on bar-sponsored Jag Wagons, the Red River Valley's original party buses.

Thirsty North Dakotans waited at the main jag wagon station in downtown

Fargo, just east of Broadway on NP Avenue. The large wagons, pulled by a single horse, offered free transportation to the Moorhead saloons day and night. Fargo city planners hoped that the new streetcars that started running in 1904 would put the ragtag party wagons out of business, but Fargo drinkers could score a free ride until 1913.

If you didn't want to wait for the jag wagon, there were dozens of bars within walking distance. While vendors in East Grand Forks tempted beer fans with saloons just over the bridge, Moorhead saloon owners built right on top of the footings of the two bridges that crossed the Red River. That must have really driven temperance advocates crazy as they passed by.

The saloons on the South Bridge (along modern Main Avenue, which was then called Front Street) were rougher and wilder, while bars on the North Bridge (the modern NP/Center Avenue bridge) were elaborately decorated. Establishments became more upscale as patrons walked away from the river and deeper into the city.

German immigrant Thomas Erdel operated two saloons, the House of Lords and Rathskeller Over the Rhine in Moorhead. The former had its own bowling alley, while the latter featured European beers, German lunches

The Conie Remley Jag Wagon. *David Remley Collection, HCSCC.*

Storehouses like the Hamm's Brewing Company storehouse in East Grand Forks supplied beer to North Dakota drinkers during Prohibition. *Alicia Underlee Nelson.*

and a swanky interior. Beer fans could belly up to the Three Orphans' forty-eight-foot-bar (the longest straight bar in the United States), relax on riverfront porches or check out the Midway, a gaudy, palatial place lit built by John Haas, nicknamed the "Dutch Prince." It was lit by four hundred electric lights and powered by its own power plant. The Moorhead bar scene welcomed all classes of men, and business was booming. Moorhead's forty-eight saloons took in $48,000 in licensing fees and fines in 1910 alone.

East Grand Forks and Moorhead were first-class party cities. But no North Dakota border town was wilder than Mondak, Montana. This rip-roaring little hamlet was built two and a half miles west of Buford, North Dakota, in 1903, literally on top of the Montana/North Dakota border.

The state line ran right down the center of at least one bar in Mondak. You'd order a beer in Montana and then walk across the room into North Dakota to drink it. Since you could drink alcohol in North Dakota, but you couldn't transport or sell it, it was all technically legal.

There were seven saloons in Mondak by 1904 and reports of as many as seventeen during the town's heyday. Mondak was also home to three wholesale brewery warehouses (including Hamm's and Schlitz) that supplied the saloons and shipped beer as far east into North Dakota as Devils Lake. Traveling hardware salesman G.E. "E" Misz reported that the saloons spent between $50,000 and $80,000 a year on alcohol, but he'd heard of expenditures topping $150,000 annually.

There were also two hotels, a few boardinghouses, a bank and a very successful red-light district on the south side of town that contained at least four but possibly as many as fifteen brothels. But getting frisky in Mondak was risky. Gunslingers offered protection to the men who sought female companionship, since many men who walked alone never came back.

This was a notoriously dangerous town, with stories of shootings and knife fights every night and one recorded lynching. The town's bad reputation attracted notice from newspapers across the nation, including the *Boston Sentinel*, which reported that Great Northern employees also had to be decent fistfighters, since brawls would break out whenever anyone tried to take tickets from the drunk men boarding at the Mondak station.

Mondak's wild run ended when Montana went dry in 1919. It's a true ghost town now, with only a few buildings and a handful of foundations that survived a prairie fire sparked by (I kid you not) a train carrying John Philip Sousa's band in 1928.

Minnesota border cities had already enacted prohibition in 1915. The entire country would go dry when the Volstead Act made prohibition the law of the land in 1920. Now beer fans all over the nation were forced to do what North Dakotans who lived far from rail lines and border cities had been doing all along: getting their beer on the black market or brewing their own.

BLIND PIGS, SPEAKEASIES AND OTHER DENS OF VICE

The name "blind pig" was a popular way to refer to an establishment that sold illegal alcohol. Operators sometimes charged an admission fee to see an attraction (like a blind pig). There was no blind pig, of course, but customers would get a few drinks for their trouble. Charging for an attraction, not the illegal hooch, meant that owners could argue (usually unsuccessfully) that they were operating legally.

Blind pigs were no-frills operations that were often found in the back of legal businesses like soda fountains, shops and billiard parlors. Many restaurants and hotels converted unused rooms into more upscale speakeasies for residents and travelers. These spots sometimes offered other illicit pleasures.

The seven-story Patterson Hotel in downtown Bismarck was the tallest building in the state when it opened on New Year's Day 1911. The gracious lobby (which now houses Peacock Alley American Grill and Bar) welcomed patrons to the 150 rooms upstairs, which were also rumored to host local prostitutes. A secret alarm system kept unwanted guests away from illegal alcohol and gambling available on the premises. Beer fans can tour the tunnels underneath the downtown streets that supplied the illicit booze.

The stories out of Minot were even more scandalous. On September 8, 1914, the *Daily Optic* reported that a prostitute was running a blind pig, brothel and opium den out of the back room of a restaurant. Other articles noted similar drug and prostitution arrests, even after Minot's red-light district on the west side of town stopped making news. Beer suddenly looked pretty tame compared with the opium, morphine, cocaine and paid female companionship widely available within the city.

Illegal alcohol wasn't just an issue in North Dakota cities. There were blind pigs in almost every North Dakota community, no matter how small. Tiny Omemee, now a true ghost town just south of the Manitoba border, never topped 650 people but still managed to support at least four blind pigs. Munich, a few miles to the east, was even smaller but boasted thirteen blind pigs and a gambling outfit that was open around the clock.

Many blind pigs operated both illegally and openly. Cowboys reported blowing a year's pay in one drunken night in Dickinson's blind pigs. Numerous firsthand accounts from Williston residents show that blind pigs there didn't even try to hide their true purpose. Patrons consumed alcohol openly, even in the middle of the day. Remote towns rarely attracted attention from the North Dakota Law Enforcement League, headed by Reverend Frank Lincoln "Shoot to Kill" Watkins (who did indeed live up to his not-so-holy nickname), so vendors kept on selling.

Even if local law enforcement was aware of illegal activity, there was often little it could do to stop it. "It is out of the question for the city of Minot to enforce the law against blind pigging with five policemen,"

The Patterson Hotel was a popular speakeasy in Bismarck. *Alicia Underlee Nelson.*

lamented Minot's mayor in 1906. The city had twenty-eight blind pigs and a sympathetic population that largely ignored the fifty-dollar reward for reporting illegal activity.

Sometimes local law enforcement and city leaders were more than sympathetic. A front-page story in the July 4, 1907 issue of the *Tolna Tribune* detailed the mysterious disappearance of five cases of beer, half stolen from the city jail and half from the private cellar where it was moved after the first theft. After a raid on Minot's blind pigs a few years later, the sergeant and the police chief both had keys to a stash of six hundred bottles of beer locked up in city hall, so it was a bit of a surprise when all but six bottles turned up empty. "The evaporation must have been great," mused the *Ward County Independent* on October 18, 1910. "Mayhap, it leaked down the throats of certain thirsty police officers, city officials or their friends."

Transcripts from the County Court of Increased Jurisdiction in Ward County show just how profitable an illegal beer business in and around Minot could be. A blind pigger testified that he sold about four barrels of beer every day. There were 72 bottles to a barrel, so he averaged around 288 bottles daily. He charged $0.35 for each bottle or three for $1.00. His net profit was six cents a bottle, or about $17.00 a day. "That sure beats threshing, don't it?" asked the folksy prosecuting attorney. It *definitely* did.

Arvid Norstrum, Gus Svenson, Francis Ringler and a fourth man pick up beer at the Binford train depot in 1918, well after it was illegal to ship beer by rail. *State Historical Society of North Dakota (SHSND), 00032-GG-16-01.*

A bottle of beer cost about 10 percent of a farm worker's daily pay. That means a farm hand made about $3.50 a day, compared to the blind pigger's $17.00-a-day profit. Getting caught was an acceptable risk.

If citizens didn't want to risk going out to drink, they could order in. Whiskey and beer distributing agents in Minot worked with eastern wholesalers who shipped alcohol to Minot by rail well after the 1913 law made it illegal. Residents placed an order under a false name, and the agent went to the depot, picked up the order and delivered it.

These weren't small orders, either. Officials seized an entire railroad car of beer and whiskey from the Soo Line Depot in downtown Minot in May 1915. When the nation went dry in 1920, this Minot depot would serve as the U.S. gateway point for Canadian alcohol from Saskatchewan, a trade controlled by legendary Chicago mob boss Al Capone.

NORTH DAKOTA'S MOB TIES AND BEER RUNNERS

Railcars full of alcohol moved from Moose Jaw, Saskatchewan, and into Minot. The contents were distributed to blind pigs in the city and across the Midwest over the Soo Line rails. The old-timers at the local bars still talk about the maze of tunnels that mobsters used to hide and move booze under the streets of downtown Minot.

Capone's shadow hangs over East Grand Forks, Minnesota, as well. The border city was an illegal booze and gambling hot spot in the 1920s and 1930s, when the sounds of slot machines could be heard pinging up and down DeMers Avenue. Both Minot and East Grand Forks earned the nickname "Little Chicago."

Most of the Chicago circuit's business involved Canadian whisky (which was much stronger and more profitable than beer), but there are stories about North Dakotans making illegal Canadian beer runs through border cities like Bottineau and Minot. Those making the midnight runs near Minot were guided by a series of house lights left blazing by cooperative farmers along the route. There are few secrets in a small town—and even fewer reasons for recreational vehicles to be out at night in the countryside—so these beer runs were probably common knowledge. The neighbors just kept their mouths shut.

Making Your Own:
Early Homebrewing in North Dakota

Prohibition made brewing beer at home illegal, but (surprise, surprise) many North Dakota beer fans didn't care. The tradition of homebrewing was another of the state's open secrets.

The supplies for creating a brewing system were available at local hardware stores. Grocery stores carried yeast, cans of malt syrup and the malt extract favored by generations of North Dakota homebrewers. Advertisements said it was used for baking, but some also contained hops—*not* a standard ingredient in cakes or cookies. Not every prairie wife with yeast and cans of malt extract in her shopping bag was baking bread.

Farmers in the region didn't need to buy malt product at all. They could malt their own barley using a process similar to the one that Albert Hoiland's father, Aadne Hoiland, used in the 1880s, as Albert explained in a WPA interview:

> *Malt for beer brewing was prepared by putting one bushel of barley in a grain sack. The sack was then tied shut, fastened to a rope and submerged in the Sheyenne River and allowed to soak for three days. This soaking so swelled the barley that it made a whole sackful. Clean cloths were now spread on the upstairs' floor when it was warm. The barley was spread on the cloth about three inches thick to sprout. When the sprouts were one inch long, the barley was put in large pans four inches deep. These were then put in the oven to dry the barley quickly. Care had to be taken in drying so that the barley did not burn, which would give a bitter taste to the beer. The dry barley, sprouts and all, was then coarsely ground on a common feedmill in Valley City.*

Once the malt was prepared, the Hoilands got ready to brew. "A 50-gallon syrup barrel was prepared in the same manner that the salt barrels were prepared for storing and leaching ashes, except that the chips were carefully selected—clean oak—and no hay was necessary," Hoiland explained.

> *The barrel was filled with round, dry malt. Boiling water was poured on the malt until the barrel was full. It was then allowed to stand for six hours. The liquid was drained off the malt in this barrel and poured into a boiler on the kitchen stove and heated to a boil. Then, enough hops were added to make a three-inch layer in the boiler. It was then boiled for 30 minutes*

during which the content were stirred constantly. Then it was strained to remove the hops. The liquid was added to that in the second barrel and brewing yeast was added. When cool, it was put into beer kegs or cider barrels which were left uncorked for three weeks. The beer was then ready to be served. It made a wholesome refreshing drink, especially in the summer, for it corrected the reactionary effect of the river water.

As the Great Depression loomed over the prairie, these traditional homebrewing techniques would still be used, but they'd no longer be necessary. After forty-three years without alcohol, the pendulum of popular opinion swung in the opposite direction. As the country faced widespread hunger and unemployment, it no longer seemed smart to spend time, energy and resources policing alcohol production.

When North Dakota voted to repeal prohibition in the state in 1932, residents were more than ready for a cold beer. The measure passed by thirty-five thousand votes.

Clarence Breker's homebrewing bottles. *Cher Spieker*.

Harvesting barley. *Jared Stober*.

Right: Glasses from the long-closed Great Northern Restaurant and Brewery still show up in local bars. *Alicia Underlee Nelson.*

Below: Brewer Michael Johnston at the Old Broadway Food and Brewing Company. *Warren Ackley.*

Brewer Joel Anderson (*left*) and owner Kirk Martinez at Rattlesnake Creek Brewery and Grill. *From the* Bismarck Tribune.

Souris River Brewing is Minot's first brewpub. *Alicia Underlee Nelson.*

A beer box from the first North Dakota brewery after Prohibition. *Alicia Underlee Nelson.*

Dakota Beer cans. *Alicia Underlee Nelson.*

Above: From left to right: Ryan Johnson, brewer Sam Corr and Drew Kelly outside Drumconrath Brewing Company. *Sam Corr.*

Left: Mike Frohlich in the Laughing Sun Brewing Company brewhouse in Bismarck. *Mike Frohlich.*

Above: Under Brew Skies in Fargo's Island Park is hosted by the North Dakota Brewers Guild. *Jesse Feigum*.

Left: A beer flight at Flatland Brewery in West Fargo. *Alicia Underlee Nelson*.

A hops tour at Ostlie's Sunnyside Acres. *Lindsey Ostlie.*

Bottles and promotional items from Dakota Brewing and Malting Company in Bismarck, from the Royce Granlund Collection. *Alicia Underlee Nelson.*

Above: Beer has been a part of ranch culture in North Dakota since before statehood. *North Dakota Tourism*.

Right: A patron enjoys a beer flight in the Fargo Brewing Company taproom. *Alicia Underlee Nelson*.

Beer fans leave their mark in the Fargo Brewing Company taproom. *Alicia Underlee Nelson.*

Two of Rhombus Guys Brewing Company's best-selling beers are available in cans. *Alicia Underlee Nelson.*

Above: Alicia Underlee Nelson.

Left: A colorful beer flight at Fargo Brewing Company. *Alicia Underlee Nelson.*

Above: A flight of beers at Kilstone Brewing. *Alicia Underlee Nelson*.

Left: A toast at Drekker Brewing Company in Fargo. *Alicia Underlee Nelson*.

Jon Walters at the Rare Beer Picnic, a craft brewery and homebrewing event in Moorhead, Minnesota. *Nick Friesen.*

Naomi Orre and Carrera Horton play bingo at Kilstone Brewing. *Alicia Underlee Nelson.*

Until 2016, much of western North Dakota considered Beaver Creek Brewery in Wibaux, Montana, to be its hometown brewery. *Alicia Underlee Nelson.*

Casks at Rhombus Guys Brewing Company in Grand Forks. *Alicia Underlee Nelson.*

Above: Junkyard Brewing Company in Fargo's sister city, Moorhead, Minnesota, is an honorary Fargo brewery. It's even a member of the North Dakota Brewers Guild. *Alicia Underlee Nelson.*

Left: These Centennial hops in North Dakota State University's variety trial will give farmers and agronomists more information about which hops grow best in North Dakota. *Kyla Splichal.*

Right: The Blue Rider was built during Minot's boozy Prohibition period. *Alicia Underlee Nelson.*

Below: The founders of Fargo Brewing Company. Left to right: John Anderson, Jared Hardy, Chris Anderson and Aaron Hill. *Aaron Hill.*

Above: Bird Dog Brewing in Mandan operates out of what may be the only drive-through taproom in the country. *Dennis Kwandt.*

Left: Aaron Pelton (*left*) and brewer Kenny Driggers pose in the brewhouse at StoneHome Brewing Company, Watford City's first brewpub. *Angie Pelton.*

Chapter 4

BEER GOES MAINSTREAM

Barn Dances, Epic Parties and the
First Post-Prohibition Brewery, 1933-1978

We are here to drink beer…and live our lives so well
that Death will tremble to take us.
—Charles Bukowski

National Prohibition ended on December 5, 1933. North Dakotans drank a lot of beer during the first years after temperance, since Congress made 3.2 percent beer legal earlier in 1933, but hard liquor would remain illegal until the state's voters passed a referendum to allow it in 1936.

Nearly two thousand businesses applied for city and state liquor licenses after prohibition was lifted. Beer had finally gone mainstream. It was sold in a variety of retail and off-sale establishments, including pool halls, hotels, nightclubs, smoke shops, bars and liquor stores in established cities as well as the newly settled small towns that popped up along the Minneapolis, St. Paul and Sault Ste. Marie (nicknamed the "Soo Line") Railroad, which cut diagonally across the state from Hankinson in the southeast to Minot in the northwest.

While some rough, frontier-style saloons still remained in western cattle country and in the most remote rural areas, bars and taverns in most cities and towns were comfortable spots located along well-traveled Main Streets and bustling city centers. For the first time in the state's history, Native Americans and women could legally belly up to the bar.

Federal law prohibited Native Americans from consuming alcohol until President Dwight Eisenhower lifted the ban in 1953. Although Native

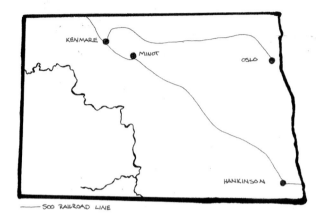

Left: The Soo Line railroad in North Dakota. *JoRelle Grover and Joseph Steinmann.*

Below: The Bismarck Tavern, one of the oldest bars in Fargo. *Alicia Underlee Nelson.*

Americans could now legally choose to have a beer, many tribal nations elected to preserve prohibition within their borders. These reservations remained dry.

Before statehood, the only "respectable" women who worked in the beer industry were the wives and daughters who served in German beer halls owned by their families. But starting in the 1930s and '40s, women could pour and serve beer without worrying about the law or their reputations. Fargo's Famous Five Spot at 205 Broadway hired the city's first female bartender in the early 1950s, while Alex Hach started a family tavern and general store in Wales, near Langdon, that his son, Amid, and daughter-in-law, Annie, turned into a thriving, reputable family business.

The Hach tavern was a typical, family-run bar except for one thing: it's unlikely the Hach family consumed alcohol themselves. Like fellow Syrian immigrant Mike Saign, who ran a tavern in the small northeastern town of Mapes, the Hachs were Muslims and avoided alcohol for religious reasons. They were part of an increasingly diverse group of saloon owners and bartenders that served their customers without getting drunk themselves. The image of a pistol-toting, hard-drinking North Dakota barkeep was a thing of the past, replaced by a more subdued professional.

Since North Dakota wouldn't have a commercial brewery in operation until 1961, most of the beer served in this era was from Budweiser, Miller or Coors or a regional brew from Hamm's, Schmidt, Grain Belt, Blatz, Pabst or Schlitz. There *was* still local beer being made in the state—it just wasn't technically legal.

Homebrewing, North Dakota's Open Secret

Homebrewing remained illegal in the state, but even the governor's wife broke the law for medicinal purposes. When Lydia Langer, wife of William Langer—the colorful, scandal-plagued seventeenth and twenty-first governor of North Dakota in the 1930s—needed to gain weight, she asked her German maid to brew homemade beer.

Most early homebrewers worked from memory, and their secrets age and pass away with them. But the brewing systems, bottles, ingredients and photos they left behind provide a few clues. The crisp, easy-drinking lagers and pale ales they produced would have been in keeping with the popular styles of the day. Most used recipes that called for malt extract or malt syrup, which was readily available at grocery stores.

Clarence Breker, a butcher and hunting outfitter in Cayuga, in the southeastern corner of the state, brewed beer using malt extract at least twice a year. His son, Joe Breker, was along for the ride when his dad got his first and favorite beer recipe from a friend in 1968. Clarence Breker liked the pale ale so much that he left with a list of supplies he needed to set up his own brewing system. He used both the recipe and the brewing system for the rest of his life. Clarence Breker was brewing his Breker beer in eight-gallon batches with the help of his grandnephew until his death in 2009.

His son, Joe, recalled his dad's brewing process. "He had two, twelve-gallon wastebaskets, and then he'd fill them up to a magic marker line. He used cans of malt extract, and he'd put a can in each one. You had to warm them up to get them to pour out. It looked like molasses syrup," Breker explained. "He'd always tell me, 'Go down and shine a flashlight in the wastebasket and tell me if there's bubbles coming up,' because that was the signal that it was time to bottle."

When the beer was ready, the elder Mr. Breker would add a pinch of sugar and a packet of header powder into each batch, which would carbonate the beverage as it aged. The beer was poured into clean, previously used bottles (almost always champagne bottles), sealed with a crimped bottle cap and stored for six months in the family's cool, unfinished basement.

Clarence Breker called his beer a pale ale. But Joe Breker said his father's brew most resembled the Standard lager from Fulton Brewery in Minneapolis. It's an all-malt beer, which fits with Joe Breker's recollection that his dad never brewed with hops.

The beer-making process was similar in nearby Wishek, according to Carmen Rath-Wald, director of the Tri-County Tourism Alliance, which preserves the cultural heritage of German Russians in McIntosh, Logan and Emmons Counties. Brewers there also used malt extract and reused bottles for their

Clarence Breker's homebrewing labels (*left*) and his grandson Phil Breker's labels (*right*). *PhotoRx.*

homebrew. "If you go to auction sales in German-Russian Country, oftentimes you'll see rusted old bottle cappers which were found in many homes," Rath-Wald said. "The bottle cappers were used on homemade beer and root beer."

Her parents, Edwin and Helen Rath, and her godparents, Violet and Waldemar Diegel, started brewing their own beer and root beer after both couples married in 1949. They kept it up until at least the 1960s. Based on Violet Diegel's memories of the taste of the beer (it was smooth and not bitter) and the fact that the couples stored the beer before drinking it, this means that they probably brewed some type of lager. The Diegels' unusual lagering process came with one particular drawback. "I remember my godparents made homemade beer once and laid the bottles up on the roof to 'cure,'" said Rath-Wald. "They had several explosions as the bottles blew up! The yeast in the beer could make the caps shoot off."

"It didn't always turn out right," laughed Violet Diegel, "but when the beer was good, it was *good*. I still wish I could taste it. I'm not a beer drinker, but the homemade beer—that was *so* good. I would just love to taste it again."

Diegel, one of the last homebrewers of her generation, grew up on a farm near Wisek. Like many of her contemporaries, she learned to brew from her parents and took this practical skill into her own home when she married. "I think we followed a recipe, but I don't have that anymore," she said. "If only we'd written these things down! Everybody knew how to do it."

The Diegels' brewing process was similar to Breker's. "We would buy the malt—we bought that in a can—and then you added water and sugar and yeast and you let it brew," Diegel explained. "We would use cake yeast.... They were like a cube, maybe a half an inch thick. You had to let it set in a crock until the fermenting was over with, and then you would bottle it. We had the deal to close the bottle and put caps on. We got our own bottles—still have them in the attic."

In the days before electricity, farm wives like Diegel had to get a little creative when it came to chilling and storing their beer. "You had no refrigerator to put it in to keep it cool," she explained. "What you did, was you sometimes took it out to the windmill and put it in a bucket in the tank. The cold water would run over the bottles and keep it cold. Oh my gosh, how different everything is nowadays!"

Homebrew was usually consumed at home with friends, family and business associates. When people did drink homebrew in public, they brought it to dances, parties, community picnics and weddings. And don't think for a minute that these parties were subdued affairs. These prairie ancestors could probably drink us all under the table.

WEDDING DANCES GONE WILD

The homebrewing Germans from Russia, the Ukrainians in the western part of North Dakota and their Bohemian neighbors from what is now the Czech Republic were famous for their wedding celebrations. Early settlers would put the furniture out on the lawn or clear out a barn or even a grain silo when it was time for a wedding.

The Bohemians in New Hradec, north of Dickinson, threw elaborate wedding parties. The food was served in the afternoon, and everybody danced and partied into the next morning. Wedding dances typically continued for two or three days, with guests sleeping on the floor as needed.

When wedding dances moved out of the home and into dance halls like the Terra Cotta Ballroom in Pisek, they were still all-day affairs. Mattern's Lounge and Blue Room (called the Blue Room today) started hosting wedding dances in Strasburg in 1946. A typical German Russian celebration started with the wedding ceremony in the morning, a light lunch and more food, drinks and dancing all afternoon and evening. There would be kegs of beer and servers with potent, homemade hochzeit schnapps circulating throughout the hall. The younger generation learned to respect alcohol and indulge responsibly early on. (And the local police looked the other way when minors were served.)

BIG BANDS, BARN DANCES
AND THE STATE'S ONLY BEER-FUELED RIOT

North Dakotans didn't wait for a special occasion to get together and dance. Ballrooms like the Blue Room also hosted public dances by national recording artists like Don Shaw, Six Fat Dutchman and the fantastically named Whoopee John. Local Bohemian bands like the Jolly Czechs, the Myron Pecka Orchestra and the Chuck Kadrmas Orchestra played at hot spots like the Eagles Club in Dickinson.

Even predominantly Norwegian towns in temperance strongholds started changing their tune. Mary Ann Johnson recalled attending regular community dances above the beer parlor in Galesburg, a small farming community in the eastern part of the state, in the mid-1930s, when she was only six or seven years old. "My dad played the violin, and another guy played the accordion," she said. "Kids were allowed. And as we got sleepy, they'd throw a coat on the floor and we'd lay on the floor and sleep a little bit."

One of North Dakota's most popular (and unusual) dance halls was located just a few minutes away, on a quiet farmstead between Arthur and Hunter. A line of headlights creeping down Highway 18 has meant the same thing since 1952: a barn dance. The state's longest-running dance hall is an actual barn, with livestock and everything.

You can still bring in coolers of beer, just like back when Herb Johnson first laid down a twenty- by thirty-five-foot wooden dance floor over the livestock pens and booked his first band. Johnson's Barn became more of a concert venue in the 1980s (it still operates as Arthur's Barn today), but in the '50s and '60s, partygoers came for Wednesday and Friday night dances that featured eight- and nine-piece orchestras, including some of the most accomplished African American performers of the era. When workers at a local cafeteria weren't sure if they should serve Preston Love and his orchestra, Johnson stormed in and insisted that the performers he brought to town deserved great service, no matter their skin color.

The times were changing in America, and the old ways of drinking and dancing didn't appeal to the next generation of North Dakotans. Homebrew was something their grandparents made, and they rolled their eyes at their parents' orchestra music. They drank beer at concerts, college bars, house parties and outdoor keggers. One party got so big that it made national news.

It all started innocently enough. Chuck Stroup, a North Dakota State University student, couldn't afford to go anywhere for spring break, so he put a satirical ad in NDSU's student newspaper, *The Spectrum*, promoting "Zip to Zap a Grand Festival of Light and Love." The festival, which wryly promised "free lovin' and smoke blowing," was slated for May 9–11, 1969, in the tiny town of Zap, about three hundred miles west of the Fargo campus. The locals in Zap were into it. The bars stocked up on beer, and the diner prepared "zapbugers" for the hungry students.

Then the Associated Press got wind of the event, and things got out of hand. The story ran in newspapers across the country. Revelers packed into their cars and streamed toward Zap from as far away as Texas and California. In an incredibly bizarre promotional tie-in, the toy company Wham-O (maker of the Hula Hoop, Slip N' Slide and the Frisbee) used the event to launch the ZipZap toy.

An estimated two to three thousand partiers packed into the bars, and owners doubled the price of beers in an effort to slow them down. They drank up the city's supply of beer anyway. Beer cans littered the sidewalks,

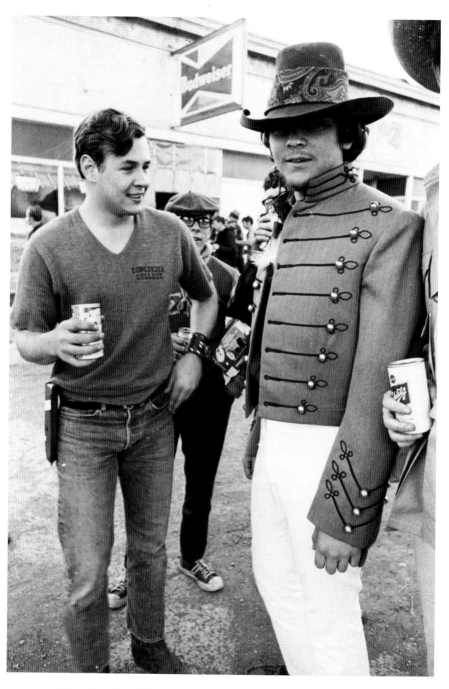

Revelers at Zip to Zap. *State Historical Society of North Dakota (SHSND), William E. (Bill) Shemorry Photograph Collection, 1-72A-2-9.*

revelers climbed on top of buildings and people started lighting bonfires. When the flames approached the power lines, the townspeople had seen enough. Many of the partygoers hadn't even arrived yet.

About one thousand revelers were passed out or sleeping when five hundred North Dakota National Guard soldiers (many of them college age themselves) arrived with bayonets to break up the party during the early morning hours on May 10. Student organizations at NDSU and UND in Grand Forks paid for $25,000 in damages. Sheepish North Dakotans watched the coverage from Zap on *CBS Evening News with Walter Cronkite* that Sunday night.

The beer cans that littered the streets of Zap were from big, national breweries. If things would have gone differently in Bismarck a few years before, the partygoers might have been drinking local beer.

North Dakota businessmen tried to harness the state's barley output for local beer production as soon as it was legal to brew after prohibition. The Capitol City Brewery Company in Bismarck was incorporated with $350,000 in capital in December 1933. A second fledgling Bismarck brewery, the Dakota Brewing Company, was founded in March 1935. Its investors brought $255,000 in operating capital to the table. In September 1935, Minot Brewing Company was founded with $200,000 in capital stock. None of these breweries made it beyond the planning stages.

DAKOTA MALTING AND BREWING COMPANY, 1959–1965

North Dakota's first brewery after the collapse of national Prohibition finally materialized when the Dakota Malting and Brewing Company was established in 1959. Much of the brewery's funding came from ordinary North Dakotans, since it sold $1 shares to bar and liquor store owners, as well as the farmers who would produce the brewery's malting barley. It reportedly raised $850,000 from 3,600 shareholders.

The company broke ground on the east side of Bismarck, at the corner of Main Avenue and Twenty-Sixth Street, in August 1960. It had the capacity to produce between 75,000 and 100,000 barrels of beer annually, making it a big player in an increasingly competitive beer market. There were just 183 breweries operating in the country in 1961.

Brewmaster Frank Bauer arrived in town with an impressive résumé. He learned the beer business by helping his father run Capital Brewing

Company in Jefferson City, Missouri, and had served as vice-president of production at the Goebel Brewery in Detroit for fifteen years. He was educated at the University of Missouri and Washington University and studied beer specifically at the Wahl Institute of Brewing in Chicago and the School of Fermentation in Copenhagen, Denmark.

The company signed with eight distributors that would move Dakota Malting and Brewing Company products (called Dakota Beer, for short) across the state. Designers created a distinctive can with vertical pinstripes and a red banner logo proclaiming that the barley in the beer was grown in North Dakota. The look was replicated on twelve-ounce, longneck glass bottles and eight-ounce grenade-shaped bottles called "stubbies" or "steinies." The brewery's hospitality room was decorated with a western theme. Sales reps peppered the state with ashtrays, cocktail napkins, church key bottle openers for the flat-top cans and other promotional trinkets.

All the pieces were in place for the launch of Dakota Malting and Brewing Company's beer. The company had a highly trained brewer, state-of-the-art facilities, a strong distribution network and a winning marketing strategy that appealed to the desire to drink local beer and support local farmers. But North Dakota's first post-Prohibition brewery was foiled by the most mundane detail: a filter.

The brewery drew the water for its beer from a deep well. The company didn't install a filter because Bauer probably assumed that any trace chemicals would boil off during the brewing process, just like they had at the other breweries he'd worked for. And most of them did. But a chemical called phenol did not.

Phenol is a volatile compound. The first batches of Dakota Beer would have been fine when they were tested in the brewery but would have started breaking down almost immediately. When drinkers tried their first taste of Dakota Beer in the summer of 1961, they were in for a nasty surprise.

The beer tasted "green," "off" and "skunky" and was almost undrinkable. North Dakotans are famously polite and taciturn (a typical expression of distaste might be an artfully arched eyebrow or an offhand, "Well, that's…different."), so such pointed criticism was a terrible sign. To make matters even worse, many of first Dakota Beer taste testers also had to sprint to the bathroom. In addition to making beer taste terrible, phenol can also cause diarrhea.

The targeted rollout was a public relations disaster. The brewery had put free beer in the hands of key drinkers like bar owners and the National Guard troops at Camp Grafton near Devils Lake and asked them to spread the word about Dakota Beer. They spread the word, that's for sure, but it wasn't the story the company wanted them to tell.

The brewery quickly recalled the bad beer and installed a filter, but the damage was done. Realizing that it had a major image problem, it bought the "Western Lager" label from a defunct brewery in Butte, Montana, and started distributing beer under that name in 1964. It sold for one dollar per six-pack and was a hit…until drinkers read the fine print on the label.

Dakota Malting and Brewing Company closed in September 1965, a victim of one brewing mistake and its customers' long memories. It was for sale to anyone who could pay the outstanding tax bill and prove that they had enough capital to get the brewery running again. There were no takers. There wouldn't be another independent brewery in North Dakota for thirty years.

Chapter 5

BREWPUBS, HOMEBREW AND NORTH DAKOTA BARLEY

Brewing Craft Beer in a Big Beer State, 1979-2008

Beer culture is a part of the world of food and drink. It's not just a commodity in cans and bottles, but has a value as an agricultural product with good ingredients.
—Michael Jackson

Dakota Malting and Brewing Company was just one of the many independent breweries across the country that closed in the 1960s and 1970s. The beer companies that thrived and expanded in this era were the ones that could efficiently package, market and distribute beer on a national scale. As the national breweries grew, regional breweries struggled to compete. The number of independent breweries continued to decrease throughout the twentieth century. As the 1970s drew to a close, only forty-four breweries remained in the United States.

Because each brewery held such a large share of the market, North Dakota passed strong franchise laws to protect the wholesalers that distributed beer in the state. Because wholesalers were small, family-run businesses that distributed just a handful of beers made by a few breweries, it would have been devastating if even one brewery signed with a competitor. These franchise laws tied a brewery to a distributor for the life of the company, an agreement that often outlived the original signers. Franchise laws also made it illegal for a brewery to bypass in-state wholesalers and distribute beer itself. Wholesalers became synonymous with the beers they sold, and drinkers were loyal to their beer and their bar.

NORTH DAKOTA BARLEY'S BIG BEER CONNECTION

For North Dakota farmers, loyalty to big beer runs deep. They don't drink a beer just because they like it. They also drank it because they grew the barley that made it.

North Dakota has been a top malting barley producer since just after Prohibition was repealed. Only Montana and Idaho challenge its dominance. According to the United States Department of Agriculture National Statistics Service, 750,000 acres of barley were planted in North Dakota in 2016—an acre measures just a little wider and a few yards shorter than a National Football League field.

That's a lot of football fields, but it's actually down a bit from 2015. This kind of fluctuation is normal, since most farmers grow barley in rotation with other crops to keep the soil in optimal condition and stagger their harvest periods (barley is harvested earlier than most crops). They may plant more wheat, soybeans, flax, corn, sugar beets, canola, sunflowers or any number of other crops after weighing international market projections, available storage space and the cost of seed, fertilizer and other expenses.

North Dakota barley production also evolves to meet the needs of the brewing industry in the United States. That brewing industry underwent major changes in the 1980s and 1990s that still affect brewers, beer drinkers and North Dakota barley farmers today.

Barley in North Dakota has been grown specifically for industrial-scale adjunct breweries (big names like Miller and Budweiser) since the mid-1940s. Barley breeding programs like the one at North Dakota State University in Fargo developed barley varieties that possessed very specific qualities to meet adjunct breweries' needs.

Unlike beer brewed according to the *Reinheitsgebot*, which only includes barley malt as a source of fermentable sugar, an adjunct beer uses both barley malt and adjunct grains as a non-barley sugar source. Recipes for adjunct beers like Miller Lite, Coors Light, Budweiser and Bud Light include "a little bit of rice, corn or corn syrup, anywhere from 15 to 50 percent, depending on the beer style," explained Dr. Richard Horsley, professor, department head and barley breeder at North Dakota State University's Department of Plant Sciences. "If you're using corn or rice in your beers, those grains are not providing any enzymes, so you have to rely on your barley," said Horsley. "So we were breeding for higher enzymes."

The majority of barley varieties developed and grown in North Dakota during the first decades of large-scale barley production were high-enzyme, six-row barley varieties for adjunct breweries. Farmers like them because they're disease resistant and have higher straw strength, which means the plant's stalks don't bend over in the wind and their heavy heads don't droop, so they're easier to harvest. The plump kernels and high protein content mean good yields and a good profit margin for the farmers who grow them.

REGIONAL MALTSTERS

As barley production in the state ramped up, the way farmers sold their crop changed too. Before statehood, farmers sold directly to their local brewery. After Prohibition, farmers sold their crop on the open market. Now, nearly all the barley in the state is contracted. Farmers pre-sell their crop to buyers (the breweries) through the malting companies that make the barley into malt for beer, entering into a contract with the buyer for the specific quantity and quality of barley. The farmer purchases certified seed and plants and fertilizes it to ensure that the barley will be suitable for malting.

Farmers deliver their harvested barley by truck to a grain elevator during specific delivery periods. They may need to store it in climate-controlled grain bins on their farms under specific, quality-preserving conditions for a period of weeks or even months. At the elevator, a technician conducts a series of tests to determine if the barley meets strict malting quality standards.

Technicians are on the lookout for vomatoxin (DON), a pathogen that develops if barley is exposed to rain during flowering. Protein and moisture levels must fall within a particular range, and the kernels of barley must be uniformly plump, intact and free of heat damage, chemical residue and insects. "You have a 1,200-bushel load of barley that weighs sixty thousand pounds, and one bug can reject the whole thing," said Travis Dagman, who farms with his wife, Dana, in southeastern North Dakota.

If the barley is approved as malting quality, the farmers get their checks. From there, barley grown by North Dakota farmers moves to malting facilities across the region, where it is made into malt using a process that, while mechanized and subject to rigorous quality standards, is still similar to the process maltsters have used for centuries.

The location of these grain elevators and malting facilities is no accident. "North Dakota is good for us because it's close," said Paul Kramer, vice-president of malt quality at Rahr Malting Company. "It's sustainable, and you don't have a lot of transportation costs, which is great because a lot of these brewers ask about the carbon footprint." In 2017, Rahr Malting Company's plant in Shakopee, Minnesota, became the largest single-site malting plant in the world. It sources about 15 million bushels of North Dakota barley per year through its malting procurement facility in Taft, just north of Hillsboro along the state's eastern border.

Before 2017, Cargill Malt in Spiritwood, near Jamestown in the central part of North Dakota, had been the largest malting plant in the world. The Spiritwood location is one of seventeen malting plants the company operates in nine countries around the world. "A plant of this size was primarily built to serve the large beer breweries in the U.S. and Mexico," explained Craig Kopp, North American regional environment health and safety manager for Cargill Malt. "We can malt about sixty-five semi-truck loads of grain per day."

Other farmers contract directly with Anheuser-Busch, which operates a malting plant across the Red River in Moorhead, Minnesota. The Moorhead plant processes almost 8 million bushels of barley per year. "Our malt goes to make pale malt for Budweiser and Bud Light," said Alan Slater, director of Midwest barley operations at Anheuser-Busch Companies Inc. "Two of the major breweries that use this barley malt are in St. Louis and Fort Collins. If you have a Budweiser or a Bud Light in North Dakota or Minnesota and you look at the label, it's likely brewed in St. Louis or Fort Collins. As consumers, you're getting it right back."

HOMEBREWING AND THE CRAFT BEER REVIVAL

Big beer ruled the nation for decades, and North Dakota farmers still supply the country's biggest breweries. But some beer fans across the country wanted to try something other than a mellow lager. They wanted to sample the beers they read about without getting a passport. They wanted to try the beer their ancestors had enjoyed. They wanted to be surprised. They could finally brew the beer they wanted to drink when President Jimmy Carter signed H.R. 1337, which made homebrewing legal on February 1, 1979.

Homebrewers dug deeper into beer history, tried a few basic beer recipes and then came up with their own. They shared their experiments with friends. Many of these creative collaborations morphed into homebrewing clubs, where members could pool their recipes and supplies and build on collective skills, knowledge and creativity. Others developed into full-fledged breweries.

Flatland Brewery in West Fargo grew out of a group of homebrewers. *Alicia Underlee Nelson.*

There were just 8 craft breweries in the nation in 1980. By 1994, there were 537. The Brewers Association defines a craft brewery as "independent" (no more than 25 percent owned by an alcohol industry interest that isn't itself a craft brewer), "traditional" (in that it brews and ferments beer from ingredients traditionally used in that beverage) and "small." But *small* is a relative term. A craft brewery needs to produce fewer than 6 million barrels of beer per year to qualify.

North Dakota's homebrewing community trained and supported the next generation of North Dakota microbrewers. Nearly every brewer at the helm of a craft brewery or brewpub in the state, from the 1990s through 2017, has had homebrewing experience. Most of them learned their craft in North Dakota. Many were members of North Dakota's homebrewing clubs.

Some of the best-known clubs throughout the years have included the Muddy River Mashers in Bismarck, the Prairie Homebrewing Companions in Fargo, the Heart River Home Brewers in Dickinson, Aurora Breweralis/Northern Lights and Bitter North Brewers in Grand

Forks and the Buffalo Brewers in Jamestown. They hosted tasting events and contests that exposed their members and the general public to a variety of beers. Regular meetings fostered a sense of community as members offered advice and feedback.

The groups also worked together to solve some of the real-world technical challenges that can emerge when brewing. "The practical, communal knowledge of how to do those things was probably lost," said Frank Clemens, a homebrewer from Jamestown who would later co-own Flatland Brewery in West Fargo. "It's one thing to read something in the book. It's another to *do* something."

The homebrewers were the perfect audience for the first commercially brewed beer produced in North Dakota in thirty years. The second North Dakota beer boom was centered on the brewpub.

The Great Northern Restaurant and Brewery (Fargo), 1995–1997

One historic building housed not one but *four* of Fargo's first brewpubs. The stately brick depot, with its trademark clock tower, is now in the National Register of Historic Places. It was built in 1906 and welcomed passengers until 1986, when Amtrak operations moved next door.

Magic City Financial Group out of Minot bought the building in 1994 and started remodeling the run-down building. The total remodeling cost topped $2 million. When the Great Northern Restaurant and Brewery finally opened in November 1995, it was at big deal. And it was also, well, *big*. The sprawling 12,680-square-foot building held a microbrewery, a new kitchen and seating for three hundred.

The brewmaster, Ray Taylor, was an experienced homebrewer who fell for craft beer on vacation and got hooked on making his own when his wife bought him a homebrewing kit in the mid-'80s. He and three friends formed the Prairie Homebrewing Companions in 1990. His assistant brewer, Dick Nilles, was a homebrewer as well. Both men were active members of the Prairie Homebrewing Companions in Fargo.

Taylor brewed four regular beers for the Great Northern Restaurant and Brewery, including its top seller, a mellow pale ale called Stationmaster Gold, a red ale and an ESB (extra special/strong bitter), a style that, despite the name, isn't particularly bitter. These brews are balanced, malt-forward beers that are easy to drink. Taylor estimated that the brewpub produced about seven hundred barrels of beer in 1996.

He also experimented with dry-hopped brews and a lemon beer for the brewery's second annual Great Northern Beer Festival in the summer of 1997. Breweries and homebrewers from states along the Great Northern's route were invited to bring their beers to be judged at the festival, which was held at Newman Outdoor Field in north Fargo.

It was one of the last events the brewery would host. It closed in mid-September 1997.

JJ's Bistro and Brewery (Fargo), 1998

The building didn't sit empty for long. Mark Nelson and Dale Anderson opened JJ's Bistro and Brewery in January 1998. Both men had extensive restaurant experience. Nelson co-owned and operated a restaurant called District 31-Victoria's in Wolverton, Minnesota, a small town located about a twenty-minute drive south of Moorhead.

Great Northern Restaurant and Brewery. *Alicia Underlee Nelson.*

The new restaurant and brewery was named for James J. Hill, the railroad mogul who had once owned the Great Northern railway outside. The menu offered light, European bistro-inspired food, including oak-roasted entrées, pasta and Mediterranean-influenced fare.

Nelson and Anderson expanded the building's seating to 350. Drinkers could order a beer at the bar, take in the railroad tracks from the first-floor dining room or get a bird's-eye view from a table on the second floor. The improvements didn't pay off. JJ's closed just six months later, in June 1998.

The Shooting Star Great Northern Restaurant and Brewery (Fargo), 1999–2001

In April 1999, investors from Minnesota decided to give the location a try. The White Earth Nation of Ojibwe already operated Shooting Star Casino, Hotel and Event Center in Mahnomen, Minnesota, about seventy miles northeast of Fargo. Newspaper accounts indicated that the new owners hoped to use the space as a staging area for bringing visitors to the Minnesota entertainment complex.

Dick Nilles, who'd served as assistant brewer under Ray Taylor in the building's original brewpub, was hired as co-brewer, sharing duties with Ryan Walker. The regular beers on tap were a Depot IPA, a popular Roundhouse red ale, the Whistle Stop Stout and a light blonde Golden Rail Ale that was similar to the easy-drinking flagship beer that Nilles had brewed with Taylor during his first stint at the brewery.

Despite the expanded beer list, the third time wasn't a charm. The Shooting Star Great Northern Restaurant and Brewery closed on February 24, 2001. The tribe continues to operate several entertainment and hotel properties in Minnesota.

The neighborhood was changing as the building sat empty. Fargo's Renaissance Zone program launched in 1999 with a goal of sparking private investment in the city center through five-year tax exemptions and tax credits for restoring historic buildings. Downtown Fargo slowly evolved from a collection of proudly dive-y bars and college party spots into a more diverse entertainment and dining neighborhood.

THE GREAT NORTHERN RESTAURANT AND BREWERY (FARGO), 2004–2005

Heather Gibb and Paul Sadosky were hopeful that the city was finally ready for a brewpub when they opened the restaurant and brewery under its original name on July 1, 2004. The pair brought both restaurant and craft brewing experience to the table.

Sadosky was the former brewmaster at Atlanta Brewing Company in his hometown. He was in Fargo to attend North Dakota State University and obtain a PhD in cereal sciences. He would serve as the head brewer and set to work getting the four brew kettles back into operation. Gibb, a native of Greenwich, Connecticut, was also a NDSU graduate student. She was studying transportation and logistics, but she'd managed Clancey's Bar & Grill in Winnipeg before moving to Fargo. She would reprise this role at the new brewpub.

Sadosky and Gibb were well aware of the challenges of running a business in such a large space, so they reduced the size of the dining area. They kept the bar at the west end and reserved the east side for live music.

The Great Northern Restaurant and Brewery was just finding its groove as a live music venue when the building's high overhead claimed another victim. Sluggish winter sales and a slew of high utility bills (including an alarming $14,000 per month heating bill) made 2005 a very unhappy new year for the ownership team. The electric company cut the lights on October 5, 2005. The business couldn't afford to turn them back on.

Employees, beer nerds and live music fans huddled around lanterns and mourned on the Great Northern Restaurant and Brewery's last night. The brewpub closed its doors with fifty-five kegs of beer languishing inside.

Sadosky and Gibb probably missed the sweet spot for downtown Fargo brewpubs by just a few years. They weren't the only ones to have this idea a few years ahead of its time. There were two other brewpubs operating in the Fargo-Moorhead Metro area in the late 1990s.

THE TRADER AND TRAPPER (MOORHEAD, MINNESOTA), 1995–1999

The region's first brewpub was located in a well-known restaurant across the river on Center Avenue in Moorhead. The Trader and Trapper (or the

T&T, as the regulars called it) had operated there since 1976. It was also a popular nightspot for metro area college students.

Ownership removed an outdoor deck, revamped the interior and added a ten-barrel brewing system during a six-month remodeling project. The Trader and Trapper's microbrewery opened on January 1, 1995. Doug Grey was the original head brewer, but Dick Nilles, who later went on to brew in the Great Northern depot building under two different owners, took over after Grey moved to Montana.

The Trader and Trapper's first taproom customers enjoyed its flagship Agassiz Amber, which remained a best-seller. The brewery also produced Pallisade Pale Ale, Golden Spike Ale and a Bruin Porter. Nilles usually had a fruit beer on tap, which rotated between raspberry, peach and black cherry.

The Trader and Trapper's beer was only available at the Moorhead taproom. The owners looked into contract-brewing its Agassiz Amber for distribution at Cold Spring Brewery in Cold Spring, Minnesota, but the plans never materialized. The restaurant and brewery both closed in 1999.

The Old Broadway Food and Brewing Company (Fargo), 1997–1999

Another brewpub opened a few blocks north of the Great Northern in 1997. The Old Broadway Food and Brewing Company was located at the corner of Broadway and NP Avenue in 1997 on one of the oldest blocks in downtown Fargo.

Owners Warren Ackley and Randy Thorson hired head brewer Michael Johnston and installed a copper and brass ten-barrel brewing system so large that they had to bring it in through the windows. Thorson also had a certificate from a brewing school in Boston, so the trio worked together on a beer list that both satisfied local tastes and differentiated their brewery from their competition. "The Great Northern Brewery and the Moorhead brewery were both open then, so we wanted to be different than them," said Ackley. "So we started brewing more mainline brews. They weren't very hoppy. Miller Lite was the king of beers at that time, so our Northern Light tasted like Miller Lite."

This strategy raised eyebrows among the local homebrewers, but the Northern Light did well, although the Brewers Blonde was the brewery's best seller, followed by a raspberry wheat, the aforementioned Northern Light, the

An Old Broadway Food and Brewing Company label doubles as wall art. *Alicia Underlee Nelson.*

River City Red and Broadway Brown. Johnston also developed an oatmeal stout and a lager. Ackley estimates that Johnston brewed about four batches a week, four days a week.

"The one mistake I made was to only have our beer on tap," said Ackley. "If I were to do it again, I would have my four beers to six beers on tap, plus six from other breweries. They had nothing to compare our beer to."

By 1999, the Old Broadway Food and Brewery was struggling. "The other two had closed by then, and we were the only brewery left," Ackley said. "And the general public felt like, 'Oh, breweries don't make it.'" The brewery portion of the business finally closed in 1999. The Old Broadway brand continues as a restaurant, club and sports bar today.

Ackley and Thorson also own several other bars and restaurants in downtown Fargo and across the state. And when the next wave of the craft beer revolution hit, they were ready. They founded JL Beers, a beer and burgers franchise that has expanded to include multiple locations across the upper Midwest.

RATTLESNAKE CREEK BREWERY AND GRILL (DICKINSON), 1995–1998

While Fargo-Moorhead brewers were challenging the way drinkers thought of beer in the eastern part of the state, Kirk and Kathy Martinez were doing the same thing out west. The Denver couple wanted to move back to Kathy's roots in Dickinson. They brainstormed ideas for a brewpub with Ken Zander, a Dickinson city commissioner during a totally North Dakota–approved activity: pheasant hunting. They opened Rattlesnake Creek Brewery and Grill just before Christmas 1995.

It was located inside a historic building at the corner of Villard and Sims Streets in downtown Dickinson. The interior included the original brick walls, oak woodwork in the second-floor loft and a tin ceiling from 1915.

Rattlesnake Creek had a seven-barrel brewhouse and a boundary-pushing menu that combined classics like ribs and steak and potatoes with Mexican food and fusion dishes for both lunch and dinner. Dickinson was recalibrating after an oil boom went bust and looking for a catalyst for investment in the city's downtown.

"They were ahead of their time a little bit in Dickinson," said Mike Frohlich, a college student who was hired to wait tables. By 1996, he was both an assistant manager and assistant brewer under head brewer Joel Anderson, a recent arrival who'd learned to homebrew while studying history and geography at the University of Northern Colorado–Greeley. He later worked at a brewpub there and researched a microbrewery in Fort Collins for his senior thesis.

Rattlesnake Creek Brewery and Grill usually had eight house-brewed beers on tap. Local tastes and the national beer scene favored more mellow beer styles, which helped beer drinkers transition into craft brews. The brewery's namesake, Rattlesnake Red, an American-style amber ale, was the most popular beer in the lineup. It and an accessible Dakota wheat beer were the first two beers on tap at the Dickinson brewpub. The Blue Hawks Extra Pale Ale (named for the Dickinson State University mascot) also sold well.

"We're constantly working on our education process," Anderson told the *Bismarck Tribune* on August 18, 1996. "Customers develop a taste, then they want to try something else." Anderson soon expanded the selection to include Chipper's Brown Ale (which was named after the owners' dog), Lodgepole Porter (named for an oil formation near Dickinson) and a Canadian golden ale. Frohlich has vivid (and cheerfully profanity-laden) memories of brewing White Butte Ale with coriander, which "smells like dirty feet" and clogged the heat exchanger with tiny seeds.

Despite his annoyance with coriander, Frohlich liked the Rattlesnake lineup. "We made pretty good beer," he recalled. "Those ingredients we're making beer with now didn't even exist in 1996." As Dickinson drinkers got used to more complex beers, the brewers nudged them toward more complex flavors. "We started up with two pounds of hops in Rattlesnake [Red] and ended up with nine pounds in it," said Frohlich. "We kind of just ramped it up a little bit."

To combat the misconception that craft beer was expensive, Rattlesnake kept its beer affordable. A sixteen-ounce pint of craft beer at Rattlesnake Creek Brewery and Grill cost two dollars in 1996, just a quarter more than a twelve-ounce bottle of beer from a national brewery. Customers could also purchase growlers (refillable to-go containers) at the brewpub.

Outside Dickinson, beer fans could try Rattlesnake Creek beer on tap at the Walrus in Bismarck, the Iron Horse in Medora and Tailgaters in Williston. Anderson also brought his beer to the Great American Beer Festival in Denver in 1997. Rattlesnake Creek Brewery and Grill wouldn't return for the next festival. The brewpub closed early in the winter of 1998.

RATTLESNAKE CREEK BREWERY AND GRILL (DICKINSON), 1998–2006

But Rattlesnake Creek Brewery and Grill wouldn't stay closed for long. Dickinson businessman Dale Tuhy, who co-owned Steffan Saw and Bike (which sold the improbable combination of chainsaws and high-end bicycles), purchased the brewpub with his father-in-law, Charles Lenamond, five months later. Tuhy's sister-in-law, Cynthia Lenamond, managed the restaurant while Tuhy took over the bar and brewery. "We changed our menu more to local tastes, more of the comfort foods—something that was more affordable," said Tuhy. A house specialty was locally sourced steak.

The beer list initially remained the same, since the beer recipes were included in the sale. In addition to the chainsaw/bike shop, Tuhy also owned a homebrewing supply store called Acme Brewing Supply, taught homebrewing classes and co-founded the Heart River Home Brewers in Dickinson. But not everything that works on a homebrewing system works on a larger scale (Tuhy said that he never did get his raspberry wheat perfect enough to sell), so he rehired Frohlich to help him work out the kinks in the brewhouse after Anderson went to law school.

Tuhy was soon developing his own recipes. His personal favorite was a malty, full-bodied porter that his regulars sometimes used for Irish Car Bomb shots. But his honey wheat, made with buckets of honey from Fetch Honey and Bees in Dickinson, was perhaps the most effective gateway beer for new craft beer drinkers. "There were people that wouldn't try the craft beer, they'd say, 'Oh that's way too heavy,'" he said. "People that wouldn't even drink beer would drink that, but we'd have to caution them because it was 8.5 percent alcohol, but just as smooth as can be."

Tuhy could brew enough beer to keep up with demand but lacked space to store it. The historic building's quirks meant that the brewhouse was on

A craft beer flight at Drekker Brewing Company in Fargo. *Alicia Underlee Nelson.*

the first floor, the fermenters on the second and the coolers were in the basement, so brewing here was especially physically taxing.

Tuhy tried to delegate, but staffing problems made it impossible. He spoke frankly about the burnout that's common in the service industry. "When you're putting in sixteen-hour days, six days a week, it kind of wears on you," he said. "And when you don't enjoy it anymore, there's no reason to do it." Rattlesnake Creek Brewery and Grill would close in 2006. It enjoyed the longest run of any brewpub in North Dakota's first wave of craft brewing activity.

NORTH DAKOTA BARLEY GOES CRAFT

While the first generation of craft breweries in North Dakota closed, the total number of craft breweries exploded across the country, reaching 1,574 in 2008. This new generation of brewers wanted different properties from their barley, and North Dakota growers and agronomists were eager to meet their needs.

Craft brewers don't typically use adjuncts in their beers. Since they don't need additional enzymes to break down adjunct grains, most craft brewers prefer two-row barley, which offers greater extract value, or more bang for their barley buck. "To the farmer, yield is bushel per acre," explained Dr. Richard Horsley. "And to the brewer, yield is extract per acre."

The major malting plants in the region responded to brewer demand and began offering contracts for the new two-row barley varieties on the market. Some of North Dakota's malted barley is bagged at Cargill Malt's Sheboygan, Wisconsin location, and distributed to craft breweries across the nation. Rahr Brewing Company's major 2017 expansion is designed to meet the increasing demand from craft brewers like Schells Brewery in New Ulm, Minnesota; Leinenkugel's in Chippewa Falls, Wisconsin; Summit Brewing Company in St. Paul, Minnesota; and more across the country.

Summit Brewing Company is actually owned and operated by a North Dakota native. Mark Stutrud grew up in Wahpeton and went to college at the University of North Dakota. He founded Summit, one of the first craft breweries in Minnesota, in 1986. His North Dakota roots (and North Dakota barley) show up in his maibock, Oktoberfest and his award-winning Summit Pilsener (which is spelled in a way that the early Czech/Bohemian immigrants in the Dakota Territory would recognize).

Stutrud brought some of his beer back to North Dakota for a family reunion in Minot in 1990. The non-drinking side of the family wasn't too thrilled about that (that pesky strain of North Dakota temperance is alive and well), so he took the keg out of the hotel bathtub and left. Distant cousin Jim Stutrud, a farmer from near Rugby, North Dakota, caught up with him the next morning, and the two started an ongoing conversation about beer. Now three generations of Stutruds—Jim; his son, Todd; and his grandson, Joshua—grow between twenty and thirty thousand bushels of Morovia 37 barley (a heritage variety with roots in the Czech Republic) per year for their cousin over in St. Paul.

Not every farmer has a family connection to a brewery, but almost every North Dakota barley producer can trace their crop's journey from their fields to the malting facility, and often to the beer, with pride. All the major malting plants offer their brewery clients the ability to trace their malt in the opposite direction.

Bismarck-based Two Track Malting Company takes traceability a step further, tracking the barley used to make its five varieties of malt right back to the exact field where the barley was planted. CEO Jared Stober can provide the company's brewing partners with detailed information on everything that can influence the flavor profile of the barley, from rainfall to the soil composition of the exact spot where the barley was grown. There are even satellite images of the fields, most of which are on the sixth-generation Stober family farm near Goodrich. Consistency is key when brewing beer, and head maltster Chris Fries wants Two Track's malt to be as consistent as possible, even before it reaches his malt house.

Two Track Malting Company is North Dakota's first craft malting outfit since before statehood. It offers a small, independent, hyper-local alternative to the regional malting plants that distribute malt to breweries around the world. The company produced five tons of malt per week in 2016 but added a second steep tank in 2017 to increase to ten to fifteen tons per batch per week to keep up with strong demand from regional breweries.

North Dakota farmers and homebrewers led the craft beer revolution after the new millennium. North Dakota barley farmers have an emotional connection to their product and close ties to the brewing industry close to home and around the world. And homebrewers wanted more complex beer closer to home. The only thing missing was a North Dakota craft brewery that could produce this beer on a larger scale. That came next.

Chapter 6

THE NORTH DAKOTA CRAFT BREWERY EXPLOSION

From Zero to a Dozen, 2009-2016

*Beer wants North Dakota just as much as North Dakotans want beer, but both
have been too damn shy to ask the other one out.*
—*Matt Charpentier*

North Dakota farmers continued to supply the nation with malting barley at the beginning of the twenty-first century, but none of it became North Dakota beer. If you wanted to buy a local pint in 2009, the closest thing you could get was a brew fermented in Fargo, made from wort trucked in from Iowa and served at a Minnesota-based chain, Granite City Food and Brewery. Brewery manager Margaret Wheeler oversees oxygenation, quality control, yeast harvesting and other brewing duties at the Fargo location, but the wort and the recipes for Granite City's flagship beers and rotating seasonal brews are the same across the United States.

It took a little longer for craft beer to catch on in lager-loving North Dakota, but once it did, it took off. North Dakota would add an average of two craft breweries every year, reaching a total of twelve operating breweries by 2016.

The explosion of independent breweries in North Dakota after the new millennium wasn't an organized movement but rather an idea that occurred to clusters of beer lovers across the state at almost the same moment. The most intense expansion period in North Dakota brewing to date was led by a motley crew of homebrewers, scientists, seasoned restaurant and bar veterans, blue-collar workers, recent college graduates and white-collar professionals. They were experienced, but they weren't experts. Only a few had brewed commercially. Most had never owned their own business. The one thing they had in common was that they all decided to make the beer they wanted to drink instead of waiting around for someone else to do it.

There was no template for this kind of business in the state, so in true North Dakota fashion, they did much of the work themselves and learned on the job. Over the course of just seven years, they educated investors, worked alongside contractors to build their taprooms and lobbied to make city and state regulations more brewery-friendly. They adjusted their recipes to a commercial scale and reintroduced their neighbors to fresh, local beer, learning from their communities and one another and recalibrating as they went.

North Dakota's third beer boom began where commercial brewing had blossomed in the years before statehood—along the banks of the Missouri. The first brewery of this new era was based in Mandan, and its beer was served in Bismarck.

THE TRAILBLAZERS: EDWINTON BREWING COMPANY (MANDAN) 2009,
WWW.EDWINTON.COM

The first craft brewery of this new era started at a Minnesota lake cabin. "It's just something we conjured up this summer," Bismarck architect David Nelson told the *Bismarck Tribune* on January 31, 2010. Nelson and his adult children had a plan for the brewery in place before they returned home from their family vacation.

The eldest son, Paul Nelson, a Minnesota chemist, started brainstorming possible beer varieties. "By the time we left, he'd already started purchasing equipment to start brewing beer," said Nelson in the *Bismarck Tribune*. His siblings divided up marketing, legal affairs and other tasks.

They called their business Edwinton Brewing Company. Although the brewery was named for Bismarck's original moniker (the city was rechristened Bismarck after German Chancellor Otto van Bismarck in an effort to attract German immigrants), the beer was actually brewed across the river in an industrial area of Mandan.

The Nelson family projected that their nanobrewery (a microbrewery that brews using a four-barrel brewing system or smaller) would produce three hundred barrels of beer a year. A target opening date was set for August

2011, but Edwinton Brewing Company faced numerous delays due to the federal approval process.

After a three-year wait, beer fans sampled the first beer brewed in North Dakota after the new millennium on October 18, 2012. It was poured at Peacock Alley American Grill and Bar in downtown Bismarck, inside the former Patterson Hotel, which had served as a speakeasy (and more) during Prohibition. The beer on tap that late fall night was called Lou, a Belgian IPA made with Citra hops. Lou and a saison called Daesy would become Edwinton Brewing Company's two flagship beers.

The company signed with McQuade Distributing in Bismarck, and by the time writer Emily Weiss swung through town to write an article for *The Growler* in 2013, its beer was also available at Reza's Pitch, a beloved Bismarck beer spot that operated until 2016. David Yaeger said the Lou was "deceptively potent" and Daesy "a honey and rosehips-infused Belgian ale that's well-hopped, a tad spicy, and highly carbonated."

Edwinton Brewing Company's Facebook page announced an extra-bitter version of Lou called Lou EB just a few days after the launch party at Peacock Alley. On November 23, 2012, the brewery unveiled a citrusy, dry-hopped Belgian IPA called Lisa on Facebook and hinted at big expansion plans on Christmas Day 2012.

Then…nothing. Just like that hot young thing who asked you out and then ghosted, Edwinton Brewing Company just sort of disappeared.

Until three years later, that is. The company's Facebook page sprang to life in late 2015, teasing beer fans with remodeling photos (but no address) and a 2016 re-launch date that never materialized. In the winter of 2016–17, the Edwinton logo appeared on Peacock Alley's website, which beer fans took as confirmation that Peacock Alley had purchased or partnered with the brand. Representatives from Edwinton Brewing Company and Peacock Alley did not respond to interview requests for this book.

The Big Dreamers: Fargo Brewing Company (Fargo), 2010,
FARGOBREWING.COM

The same summer that the Nelson family created Edwinton Brewing Company, two brothers and a pair of childhood friends were also dreaming about starting a brewery. This quartet just didn't know one another yet. A chance encounter in downtown Fargo would change that.

Jared Hardy was back in town after getting his MBA at Portland University, and he already missed the Pacific Northwest's beer scene. His high school friend Aaron Hill shared Hardy's passion for good beer. They met up at a Red Hawks baseball game in Fargo and hatched a plan to open their own craft brewery. Hardy drew up a business plan, and Hill used his sales and marketing background to recruit investors. The only problem? Neither of them knew how to brew beer.

When Hardy sat down with friends at the Hotel Donaldson one fateful day in December, the beer gods handed him a solution. His server was John Anderson, a beer fan and service industry veteran who just happened to have an older brother, Chris Anderson, who knew how to brew. "We called it the 'Christmas beeracle,'" said Hill. "It's a crazy story. We had the same vision for what we wanted to do. They knew the brewing background and operations side of it, and Jared and I had the business background, so the four of us partnered up."

Chris Anderson moved back home from Washington, where he'd worked as a marine biologist and sharpened his brewing skills at Ice Harbor Brewing in Kennewick. The four partners established Fargo Brewing Company in early 2010 and started brewing in Hardy's garage. The company did business as Fargo Beer Company back then because the first batches of beer were contract-brewed at Sand Creek Brewery in Black River Falls, Wisconsin. Federal ordinances prohibited them from using the word *brewery* in their name until they were producing beer on North Dakota soil.

Unlike Edwinton Brewing Company, which intended to stay small and local, the four co-owners in Fargo had their sights set on widespread regional distribution from the very beginning. Fargo Beer Company products hit the Fargo-Moorhead market in 2011 and were distributed in the nearby Minnesota lakes region and across North Dakota shortly thereafter.

Operations moved to a low-slung cinderblock building near downtown Fargo in the spring of 2013. A new twenty-barrel brewing system (and a one-barrel setup for Chris Anderson's taproom experiments) arrived from Portland, and the company began using its legal name, Fargo Brewing Company. The taproom, production brewery and canning facility were opened to the public in the summer of 2013.

The taproom has a laid-back, industrial vibe, and customers can sneak a peek at the brewhouse from the heavily graffitied picnic tables. There are twelve beers on tap and a food truck out front for much of the year. Fargo Brewing Company also opened a pop-up taproom in downtown Fargo during the summer of 2016 and expanded to a second permanent taproom location, the Fargo Brewing Company Ale House, in September of the same year. The Ale House offers the company's beer and a focused brewpub menu featuring food inspired by and flavored with the company's beer.

Fargo Brewing Company's two best-known beers have been part of the lineup since the beginning. The malty and mellow Stone's Throw Scottish Ale is a popular gateway beer for new craft beer fans and outsells other Fargo Brewing Company beers by a landslide. Woodchipper IPA's hoppy, piney bite delights hop heads and references the movie *Fargo*. It's also a popular souvenir. It's a little weird to commemorate a trip to Fargo with a beer named for an object associated with murder, but the tourists who make it to Fargo clearly share North Dakotans' dark sense of humor.

Food truck grub and a beer at Fargo Brewing Company. *Alicia Underlee Nelson.*

After a few months in the brewhouse, Chris Anderson started playing with barrel aging and infusions, turning out taproom favorites like a brown ale with pureed raspberries called Snozbeer (named with a wink and a nudge for Willy Wonka fans) and Iron Horse with mango. Future projects include a line of sours and a lemon-infused radler, a light, summery beer most American beer fans call a shandy.

Fargo Brewing Company was one of the first North Dakota breweries to use locally sourced ingredients. Super Green, a wet-hopped pale ale, uses malt from Two Track Malting Company and whole-cone hops from Ostlie's Sunnyside Acres near Carrington and ND Hops near Minot.

The brewery has expanded steadily since its conception, distributing its beer across North Dakota, Minnesota, South Dakota and western Wisconsin. It aims to produce ten thousand barrels a year by 2021.

While Fargo Brewing Company was getting established, four other North Dakota breweries were filing the paperwork to join them. For the next few years, brewing activity was concentrated in the central part of the state.

Although Fargo Brewing Company and Edwinton Brewing Company produced beer earlier, it was a Bismarck brewery that opened the state's first post-millennium taproom.

THE ARTISTS AND ADVOCATES: LAUGHING SUN BREWING COMPANY (BISMARCK), 2012, LAUGHINGSUNBREWING.COM

Laughing Sun Brewing Company owes its existence to the band the Lost Horses. Attorney Todd Sattler and web designer Mike Frohlich went to check out their mutual friends' band at the Corral Bar in Bismarck and wound up talking about beer. Sattler had been a homebrewer since learning the craft from his dad in the 1980s. And Frohlich, as we've already learned, got his start at Rattlesnake Brewery and Grill in Dickinson. He was a co-founder of the Muddy River Mashers homebrewing club and looking for a partner to form a brewery.

Sattler and Frohlich founded Laughing Sun Brewing Company in 2012. They found the perfect taproom space in the historic Laskin Building in Bismarck's reenergized downtown district. The state's first taproom of the twenty-first century celebrated its grand opening on November 9, 2012. The 3.5-barrel brewery started with five beers. Several of those early beers are still Laughing Sun flagships.

"Feast Like a Sultan is my baby," Frohlich said, adding that he brewed the hoppy IPA specifically to pack in all the tropical fruit and grapefruit flavors that he loves. This beer, along with Fargo Brewing Company's Woodchipper IPA, put North Dakota IPAs—and craft beer in general—on the map. The brewery's other original recipes—including a biscuity, medium-hopped Hammerhead Red ESB and a rich, chocolatey Black Shox porter—still sell well. Sinister Pear, a wickedly flavorful Belgian golden strong ale, became a classic.

After years of gradually nudging drinkers out of their comfort zones with accessible ambers and ales at Rattlesnake Creek, Frohlich wanted to do something different at his own place. Frohlich is a mellow, amiable guy, but he gets fired up when he talks about how North Dakota beer has evolved.

"We don't make *anything* tamed down for North Dakota's palate," he said emphatically. "There's definitely enough of a sophisticated palate, for sure. Then, people were not nearly as adventurous. Today, we're brewing with anything you can possibly think of: chocolate, berries, peppers."

Many of these ingredients are locally sourced. Laughing Sun sources malt from nearby Two Track Malting Company and uses locally grown aronia berries, cherries and chokecherries in its 19th Amendment Chocolate Chokecherry Stout. "I'll make as much beer with local ingredients as I can," Frohlich said. "If you start talking to people about North Dakota ingredients, they want to try it."

Frohlich likes the creative challenges of brewing (this is a man who brewed a steinbier with campfire stones at nearby Cross Ranch State Park), and Laughing Sun's long, narrow taproom and lively sidewalk patio are a magnet for fellow artists, creatives and thinkers, which is appropriate, since the space used to be a gallery and frame shop. There's live music on a tiny stage and art from local artists on the walls.

Sattler and Frohlich are also two of the state's most outspoken beer policy wonks. They (along with Fargo Brewing Company) lobbied for craft beer-friendly legislation, including the 2013 taproom license that "allowed for the creation of a taproom brewery that could that could produce twenty five thousand barrels of beer annually, and self-distribute ten thousand of those barrels," explained Frohlich. This legislation permitted North Dakota breweries to increase production and sell twelve-ounce through one-sixth-barrel containers from their taprooms.

The brewery was a founding member of the North Dakota Brewers Guild, created in the summer of 2013. The guild amended the taproom license to allow for multiple taproom locations in 2015.

Laughing Sun Brewing Company currently produces 550 barrels a year and distributes in the Bismarck-Mandan community, as well as in Minot, Fargo and Jamestown. Production capacity is limited (a much-publicized second location in Mandan fell through in 2016), but Frohlich doesn't mind. "I would rather not create an empire, and have no desire to become a regional brewery," he said. "We are simply trying to create the best beer possible and be where we want to be financially."

As Laughing Sun developed a following in Bismarck, two other North Dakota breweries were exploring their options just up Highway 83 in Minot. Only one would welcome customers, but both would become players in the city's craft beer scene.

THE CONNOISSEURS: LITTLE DEEP BREWING COMPANY (MINOT), ON HOLD

Minot homebrewer Jon Lakoduk and his childhood friend Andrew Walter planned to open Minot's first craft brewery in 2011. They called it Little Deep Brewing Company, after the Little Deep Creek that runs by the Walter family farm. But shortly after Walter completed brewing school, love called him away from North Dakota. So, Jon Lakoduk recruited his brother Jordon Lakoduk, who owned a web-based business, and went with Plan B.

They wanted to brew in the Soo Line depot in downtown Minot, the spot where beer fans picked up their orders during Prohibition. But the building would have required $500,000 in structural improvements to accommodate the brewing equipment on top of other brewery expenses, and the investors got skittish.

So, the Lakoduk brothers and brewer Adam Laudenschlager implemented Plan C. They changed the name to Little Deep Beer Company, began a crowdfunding campaign and searched for a brewery to contract-brew their two beers, a California common style and an IPA. But the fundraising campaign fell short, and brewery plans were placed on hold.

But Jon Lakoduk wasn't done with beer. He became the second person in North Dakota to become a certified cicerone (like a sommelier, just for beer) and parlayed his passion into running the Taproom, a craft-only beer bar in downtown Minot.

The first attempt at a brewery in Minot didn't stick. But the second one did and endures today.

THE LOCAVORES: SOURIS RIVER BREWING (MINOT), 2012,
SOURISRIVERBREWING.COM

Souris River Brewing quietly opened in downtown Minot in December 2012 and celebrated a more public unveiling on January 6, 2013. The restaurant and brewery was the brainchild of Aaron Thompson. Nick Holwegner was the brewmaster and Daniel Haff oversaw the kitchen. Souris River Brewing (or, as the locals call it, SRB) became a cornerstone of its downtown neighborhood, which was rebuilding after the Souris River (known locally as Mouse River) flood of 2011. The Magic City was

Even the signage at Souris River Brewing has a rustic appeal. *Alicia Underlee Nelson.*

reimagining itself in 2012 and 2013, and Souris River Brewing was right in the thick of it.

Minot is a laid-back little city with a thriving art scene, a busy air force base, traffic from the oilfields to the west and a diverse group of students and professors at Minot State University. Souris River Brewing—with its church pew seating, reclaimed wood accents and curvy bar—is a low-key hangout for these disparate groups. Families gather for the evening meal, while the late-night crowd trickles in to hear live music after the sun goes down.

Souris River Brewing's menu emphasizes locally sourced food and from-scratch cooking. This isn't a particularly revolutionary concept, but it did push boundaries in a city (and a state) with a thing for chain restaurants when it first opened. SRB's food honors the region's love of meat and potatoes but nudges diners out of their comfort zone with North Dakota–raised beef, elk and bison and welcomes vegetarians with a surprising number of meat-free options. (This is one of the few spots to find kale in west-central North Dakota.)

In addition to sourcing local ingredients for the kitchen, Souris River Brewing was one of the first breweries in the state to use local hops, promoting its use of fresh hops from Laurie and Dale Dannewitz's White

Earth Hops Farm way back in 2013. Hops from the farm are still used in the Harvestfest Hopburst IPA today. Crowd-pleasing, easy-drinking beers like East Brown & Down, Souris River Swill and an American pale ale (APA) called Avram American Ale were soon joined by more esoteric offerings like Full Melon Jacket (a watermelon wheat) and a coconut brown ale called Coconut Telegraph.

Aaron Thompson bought out Holwegner, Haff and five other silent partners and recruited Dr. Bryan Schmidt as head brewer in June 2016. The beer list has been steadily expanding ever since. "We have forty different styles of beer, from the niche-iest style of beer to beer for the masses," said Thompson.

"We have IPAs, we'll have American pale ales, but we're also having a lot of British- and Belgian-style beers," added Schmidt. "More lagers, more German styles—a lot more options that people don't commonly see." The Bakken Brown Ale is a best-seller, but new flavors (and higher alcohol content) in beers like the slightly spicy Sunburst Saison and Wicked River Weizenbock are getting customers excited. Four SRB brews clock in at 9.5 percent ABV or higher: the Doctor Belgian Tripel (9.5 percent), Trainwreck

Dr. Bryan Schmidt by his yeast cooler. *Alicia Underlee Nelson.*

Tripel IPA (10.5 percent), the Executive Chef Imperial Porter (10.5 percent) and the Professor Belgian Dark Strong Ale (12 percent)—the most high-gravity beers of any brewery in North Dakota.

Schmidt has homebrewed for twenty years, and his palate and perspective evolved with him as he experimented and traveled. "But the real thing that makes me different is that I have a PhD in biochemistry," said Schmidt, in his characteristically direct style. "I've been professionally growing yeast for ten years. It actually gives us a competitive advantage here. Big macrobreweries like Budweiser pay someone like me. A craft brewery can't afford it."

When Schmidt isn't teaching at Minot State, he's in the brewhouse, developing recipes to highlight the unique characteristics of the roughly twenty-five yeast strains on hand at any given time. Souris River Brewing's beer is available throughout western and central North Dakota. The brewery has steadily ramped up production and aims to reach 1,500 barrels a year by 2021. "We're gonna continue to market ourselves to western North Dakota, the oil producing, farming crowd," said Thompson. "We're gonna grow as the state grows."

While Souris River Brewing anchored the Minot craft beer scene, three more breweries took root in the state. The next city to see a craft brewing resurgence was Mandan.

THE SOLO ACT: BUFFALO COMMONS BREWING COMPANY (MANDAN), 2012, BUFFALOCOMMONSBEER.COM

Buffalo Commons Brewing Company's Mandan taproom is as unassuming as the city itself. It's so unassuming, in fact, that's it's tricky to find if you're unfamiliar with the industrial neighborhood where it's located.

Like residents of other sister cities, folks in Mandan are used to being underestimated. If Bismarck is the smartypants older sister having a beer at a funky downtown spot after work at the capitol, Mandan works at the refinery in town or maybe the night shift at the hospital. She's not as glamorous as her big sister, but she's the girl you call when your car stalls out in the Buffalo Commons parking lot. Heck, she's probably already there, talking to brewer and owner Ted Hoffman about his newest creation.

Hoffman designed Buffalo Commons Brewing Company's production brewery and taproom to be a quiet, no-frills environment. "I think people

Ted Hoffman in the taproom. *Alicia Underlee Nelson.*

like it here because they like this kind of laid-back atmosphere," he said. "There's no TVs. We've got a small radio that you can barely hear once it's on. It's just a place where people like to sit and talk without a lot else going on."

Drinking at Buffalo Commons is like having a beer in your buddy's spotlessly clean shop or garage—one that just happens to be located in the middle of a working brewery. The taproom isn't industrial chic, but an actual, functional industrial building. When Hoffman grabs you a beer, he pours it into a plastic cup. This is not the place to wax poetic about glassware, so just sit back and enjoy your drink like a good (or honorary) North Dakotan. If you needed a tulip glass to enjoy Hoffman's beer, he would have given you one.

Like many of North Dakota's latest wave of brewery owners, Hoffman got his start at home when his wife, Linda, bought him a homebrew kit in the early '90s. He established Buffalo Commons Brewing Company in 2012. The name is a cheeky response to a pair of academics who proposed that the plains states with declining populations (like pre–oil boom North Dakota) could revert back to buffalo grazing land. (Do *not* mention this idea in North Dakota unless you want to tick everybody off.)

Hoffman brewed his first commercial batch of Salem Sue Stout on January 28, 2013, and his beer was distributed just weeks later. Mandan's newest brewery officially debuted on March 7, 2013, when Peacock Alley hosted a release party. Press for the event promised four beers on tap, including the aforementioned stout, Northern Border Pale Ale, Buffalo Commons Brown Ale and Windblown Wheat.

This early beer list is a great example of the beer that Hoffman still brews. While other breweries in the state were challenging drinkers with Belgian beers and bold IPAs, Hoffman exposed his customers to subtler flavors. Salem Sue, named for the world's largest sculpture of a Holstein cow (yep, seriously) in New Salem, North Dakota, and his brown ale are still best-sellers. Over time, he added more complex varieties like Bully! Imperial Stout and A Sour With No Name, a cloudy Berliner weisse.

By the time the Buffalo Commons Brewing Company's taproom had opened for tours, tastings and growler fills in March 2014, Hoffman could already see the local beer scene changing. "People are willing to try more things. There's more local acceptance of local beers. People are getting over the idea that if a beer isn't made by Anheuser-Busch, that doesn't mean that it's made in somebody's bathtub in the dark of night," he said with a rueful laugh.

Hoffman hopes to be operating at or near his 1,800-barrel annual capacity by 2020. [He's shifting to using more craft malt from Two Track in beers like his Honey Blond Ale, which also features honey from Bismarck's Stewart Apiaries. Plans for sourcing local hops are in the works, too. He'd also like to add a canning line at some point, but he's okay with taking it slow. Unlike some of the other breweries in the state, Buffalo Commons Brewing Company is largely a one-man show. Hoffman is content to let the brewery evolve at its own pace and provide his customers a quiet spot to enjoy a beer.

The Community Builders: Drekker Brewing Company (Fargo), 2012,
Drekkerbrewing.com

When the guys at Drekker Brewing Company talk about beer, they don't just talk about what their beer *is*. They talk about what the beer *does*.

"One of the most beautiful things about craft beer is that community and camaraderie of sharing a pint. And if we're gonna be the center of that table, we're gonna make sure the beer is up to that occasion," said Mark Bjornstad, the company's president. "That's what's really fun, when we get to find new ways to share beer with people and to create more great moments around beer."

Connecting people over a pint has been built into Drekker Brewing Company's mission since day one. It hosts late-night crafting sessions, movie nights and yoga classes and offers drinkers a chance to give back to local nonprofit organizations with its Unpillage happy hours and events.

The brewery itself was born over beers in 2012. The four co-owners—
Bjornstad and brothers Darin (the head brewer) and Mason Montplaisir
(the engineer and quality control guy), as well as Jesse Feigum (marketing,
accounting and assorted office tasks)—started homebrewing together in a
garage and first shared their beer with friends during a fall beer tasting party.

The group signed a lease on a storefront in a brand-new building in
downtown Fargo in January 2014 and transformed the 5,200-square-foot
blank canvas into a welcoming taproom and brewery. They did a lot of the
work themselves, picking up paint brushes, sanding reclaimed wood from a
friend's barn and even creating some of the art that hangs on the walls. The
taproom opened to the public in the fall of 2014.

They called their company Drekker, an admittedly made-up word that
appeals to the region's Norwegian roots and riffs on several Old Norse words,
including *drekka* (to drink), *drykkr* (a draft drink) and *drakkar* (the name for a
Viking ship). Norse images, fanciful legends and gleeful Viking wordplay pop
up everywhere in this world they've created, including on the beer menu.

Drekker Brewing Company currently rotates fourteen beers in the taproom.
Its six year-round brews, the Pillager porter (approachable, despite its name),
a malty Black IPA called Igor's Horn, the Burn the Boats American IPA, a

Tours at Drekker Brewing Company include beer samples. *Alicia Underlee Nelson.*

crowd-pleasing Irish red, a refreshing American wheat and Azacca Attacka, a single-hop pale ale that showcases Azacca hops, have been available in the taproom since day one. The Broken Rudder Irish Red, with its subtly sweet caramel notes, remains the brewery's best-seller both in the taproom and at more than one hundred locations throughout North Dakota and Minnesota.

The brewery's newest flagship, a kettle soured Berliner weisse called Techno Viking, was added to the lineup based on sheer customer demand. Darin Montplaisir also added other sour experiments—like HopTronic, an ale that features Nelson Sauvin and Mosaic hops, and Drive-By Glitter Bomb, a kettle-soured saison—to the rotation.

Most of the malt in Drekker beers come from Rahr Malting Company, so there's likely a lot of North Dakota barley in its brews. Drekker also sources ingredients from its neighbors, using coffee beans roasted by downtown Fargo's 20 Below Coffee Company for its coffee-infused Roastmaster Series and featuring farmers' market pie pumpkins in its fall pumpkin ale.

The company has already outgrown its 2015 expansion, so it's ramping up production to three thousand barrels a year. The revised five-year plan includes expanding distribution into South Dakota and deeper into North

Andrea Williams at the Red River Market in Fargo. *Alicia Underlee Nelson.*

Dakota and Minnesota. Broken Rudder and creamy, chocolately Iron Maiden were the first beers released in twenty-two-ounce bomber bottles in late 2016, and a new canning line brought cans to the Drekker Brewing Company lineup in mid-2017.

The Teacher: Bird Dog Brewing (Mandan), 2013,
BIRDDOGBREWING.BEER

Beer fans in Mandan rejoiced when Dennis Kwandt announced the pending arrival of Bird Dog Brewing in December 2013. A stout and a cider ale were available on tap at Mandan's Main Street Drive Thru Liquor at precisely 12:01 a.m. on New Year's Day 2014, so customers could ring in the new year with a local brew.

If the name "Main Street Drive Thru Liquor" didn't immediately catch your attention, it *should*. This is a weirdly wonderful spot to grab a beer. For one thing, there's a drive-through window. It's mostly used for customers who want to order coffee. (Because why *wouldn't* there be an in-house coffee shop?) But you can also get beer along with your latte. This feature exists because this building was once a McDonald's. And because using things up before you replace them is a North Dakota virtue, some parts of the building feel like a McDonald's time warp after a few beers.

The unusual setup is actually a pretty great fit for Bird Dog Brewing. The adjacent bar serves as the brewery's taproom, and Kwandt's 3.5-barrel system is nestled in the back. Bird Dog beer is on tap elsewhere in Bismarck-Mandan, but you'll find the largest variety—four tap lines—here. Kwandt doesn't have to worry about staffing the bar, but he always tries to drop by the taproom on Tuesdays.

On the second Tuesday of every month, Kwandt brings out a homebrewing system and teaches everyone to make beer on Brewer's Night. Kwandt sees himself as an educator, so events like this and the intimate taproom suit him and his clientele. "The biggest benefit is that I can talk to the customers directly," he said. "A lot of our normal customers are at the beginning of their journey, and they're learning how the different flavors come in."

Kwandt learned in much the same way. He's a veteran homebrewer and a longtime member of Bismarck's Muddy River Mashers. His beer list has grown to include seventeen brews in a wide range of styles, from the fruity, full-bodied Heart River Stout to the spicy, hazy Gordy's Harvest Wheat.

His Bourbon Barrel Porter, deep red Hunter's Amber and a honey-tinged Belgian blonde are his most popular brews.

But no matter what he's working on, one thing is consistent. "I personally tend to brew maltier stuff," he said. "Even the IPAs and the hoppy stuff I brew tends to be balanced with the malt."

He's experimenting with craft malt from Two Track Malting Company for a more local touch and exploring the earthy, floral notes of English hops. He's also revamping some old favorites, retooling that first apple cider beer into an Apple Pie Ale that features apples picked from his mother-in-law's apple trees.

He'll be making a little more of all of his beers in the future. He quit his day job as a construction designer in August 2016 and is slowly transitioning into brewing full time. Bird Dog Brewing only produced fifty barrels in its first year, but Kwandt plans to hit two hundred this year and keep increasing from there. Eventually, he might even get his own place. But for now, he's good, brewing beer at what just might be the only drive-through coffee shop/liquor store/taproom in the nation.

The Family Business: Kilstone Brewing (Fargo), 2015
FACEBOOK.COM/KILSTONEBREWING

Customers in Fargo taprooms might have noticed two particularly curious beer fans asking lots of questions in 2014. Brothers Brock and Grant Wigen went into the beer business with their dad, homebrewer Randy Wigen, and learned the ropes at Echo Brewing Company in Fairbault, Colorado. But they agree that support from the local breweries that came before them has been key to building their business. "I love the Fargo-Moorhead brewing scene," said Grant Wigen, the chattier of the two extravagantly bearded Wigen brothers. "It's a tightknit community. We all work well together to try to help each other out and promote each other's business."

The Wigen family opened Kilstone Brewing in March 2015. It was the seventh brewery operating in the state and the third taproom to open in Fargo in as many years. The taproom and production brewery are located in an industrial part of Fargo, just off (but not accessible from) Interstate 29, which runs north to Winnipeg and south to Sioux Falls, South Dakota. It's a proudly blue-collar joint that pulls in workers from the industrial park, a

Brock and Grant Wigen in the taproom.
Alicia Underlee Nelson.

residential neighborhood to the east and a truck stop to the north.

The décor is masculine and minimal. The brewers' cousin and uncle made the handsome wood bar themselves. "Artguy" Chuck Hues, a family friend, painted a large, nature-themed mural on the beer cooler behind the bar where operations manager Fallon Blank holds court, pouring beers and leading game nights. They open up the garage door when the weather's nice so customers can hang out in the parking lot turned patio. The beer flights are served on trays in mini mason jars in a way that doesn't feel precious, just practical.

The vibe is as low key as the beer on tap. "Approachable is my first word," said Grant Wigen. "We try to have fun and experiment a little bit, but we always like to have something on tap for everybody so your standard Miller and Bud Light drinker can come in and find something."

Hopposable Thumbs IPA has a subtle bite, the flagship Polyphonic Pale Ale's Cascade hops read crisp and clean and Carl's Cascadian Dark Ale features Cascade hops that their buddy Carl grows in his yard. But overall, the Wigen brothers play with quieter flavors, layering malty, bready notes and a subtle sweetness that a lot of their beers share. The Crooked Captain Caramel ESB, with its smooth caramel notes, is a good example of what they do well. So is the brewery's second flagship beer, the mellow and slightly nutty Ironstone Irish Red.

"Mellow and slightly nutty" might be a good way to describe the mood in the brewhouse most days, too. The Wigen brothers are pretty chill guys, except when they're unwinding with some brewhouse experiments (bacon amber ale comes to mind), riffing with the local classic rock radio DJs or doing a cartwheel contest after checking the quality of their Brockwork Orange Belgian Golden Strong that, at 10.5 percent ABV, is more potent than pretty much anything else on the Kilstone menu.

"We serve that in half pints and limit customers to three so they can still function," said Blank, explaining that they learned their lesson the

Beer flight at Kilstone Brewing. *Alicia Underlee Nelson.*

hard way after the aforementioned gymnastic free-for-all. (Grant Wigen still insists that he won, a heady victory fueled by the beer that bears his brother's name.)

Taproom customers can get inside the brewhouse with the Wigens during popular brewing events. But it's getting a little tight in the brewhouse, even before the visitors arrive. "We've outgrown this location already," Grant Wigen explained. "I literally have a tank sitting in the middle of the floor right now. So we're looking at a bigger system and a new location."

They're currently brewing on a two-barrel system, producing just under five hundred barrels a year. The five-year plan includes expanding to a ten- or fifteen-barrel brewing system, which would supply the taproom and expand distribution as needed. "In five years, we're also gonna have matching Kilstone crest tattoos," marketing coordinator Paul Hankel adds earnestly, his eyes wide. There's a long pause. Then the entire group bursts out laughing.

The Showmen: Rhombus Guys Brewing Company (Grand Forks), 2015, RHOMBUSGUYSBREWING.COM

If Kilstone Brewing has one of the more unassuming taproom exteriors in the state, Rhombus Guys Brewing Company has the most extravagant. Built in 1890, the brewery's stately brick building in downtown Grand Forks was once called the most prestigious opera house between Minneapolis and Seattle. The former Metropolitan Opera House is now in the National Register of Historic Places.

The building suffered heavy damage during the historic Red River flood, which gutted much of downtown Grand Forks in 1997. Floodwaters reached almost to the arches over the front door. A group of investors purchased the building during the subsequent rebuilding period, investing $3.5 million in private funds and $600,000 in Community Block Grants.

The upper levels were converted into lofts, but the ground floor stood empty until owners Matt Winjum and Arron Hendricks reimagined the five-thousand-square-foot space as a brewpub. The stripped-down interior exposes the blond brick and the building's structural elements. Natural light pours through the tall windows and back into the far reaches of the building.

Winjum and Hendricks are friends, homebrewers and business partners who have been running restaurants and food businesses in North Dakota and Minnesota since 2000. Rhombus Guys, the duo's quirky, craft beer–friendly pizza joint, has been a Grand Forks fixture since 2007. They also operate a Rhombus Guys in Fargo and Rhombus House of Pizza in Mentor, Minnesota.

But the new brewery, which opened in September 2015, offered a very different dining experience. Its menu of pub food classics (think fish and chips, shrimp and grits, addictive Scotch eggs and made-from-scratch pretzels) was designed to highlight the flavors of the beers brewed on site.

The owners recruited head brewer Chad Gunderson, a former UND student, who returned to town in January 2015 to start working on recipes. In addition to being a homebrewer like Winjum and Hendricks, Gunderson also had extensive commercial brewing experience. He'd worked at Leech Lake Brewing Company in Walker, Minnesota (now closed), and Lewis and Clark Brewery in Helena, Montana, before serving as head brewer at Mighty Mo Brewing Company in Great Falls, Montana.

The trio held focus groups and blind taste tests to come up with a beer lineup that would appeal to both craft beer fans and folks Gunderson affectionately calls "yellow beer drinkers." "We're not in the business of creating high ABV or wacky beer styles in this location. We want it to be a communal, social aspect where you can have one or two pints with friends," he said. "We make traditional ales and lagers. I try to produce a standard lineup that you know when you walk into the restaurant or when you have a Rhombus beer, it's going to be sessionable, it's going to be true to style and it's going to be consistent wherever you get it."

Most of the beer names reference the brewery's opera house past. The Illusion Amber pays tribute to illusionist Harry Houdini, who once performed at the venue, while the barrel-aged Freak Show strong ale hints at the vaudeville acts that once graced the stage. Rhombus Guys Brewing Company debuted with six beers, including Into the Darkness Brown Porter, a wheat ale called Doc's Orders, Encore IPA and the Iconic Blonde ale.

The Iconic Blonde and Invincible pale ale would be the first Rhombus Guys beers to hit liquor store shelves in cans and quickly established themselves as signature brews. Rhombus Guys beer is distributed across eastern North Dakota and will be available in selected Minnesota markets, including the northwestern corner of the state and the Twins Cities Metro Area, in 2017.

Rhombus Guys Brewing Company. *Alicia Underlee Nelson.*

The brewery sources ingredients from North Dakota and Minnesota whenever it can. The bulk of Rhombus Guys Brewing Company's malting barley comes from Cargill Malt, but the brewery also works with Vertical Malt, a craft malting operation in Fisher, Minnesota.

Jacob Hamilton replaced Gunderson as head brewer in 2017. Hamilton's resume is a North Dakota–approved mix of professional and hands-on experience. He studied brewing at Siebel Institute of Technology in Chicago, obtained a certificate from the American Brewers Guild, experimented with homebrewing and worked his way up from cellarman to head brewer at Mankato Brewing.

Rhombus Guys Brewing Company's 15-barrel brewhouse has five 30-barrel fermenters and a 30-barrel brite tank, which allows Hamilton to increase production from the 1,200 barrels produced in its first year to closer to 3,500 barrels annually. Growth is the goal. "Hopefully we'll expand our territory more into western North Dakota and continue to grow the taproom side of it," said Hendricks. "We're not in South Dakota at all yet, so that would seem like the next logical step."

The Hive Mind: Flatland Brewery, 2016,
FLATLANDBREWERY.COM

As Rhombus Guys Brewing Company hit its stride in Grand Forks, the Fargo-Moorhead brewing community welcomed another member. And West Fargo, Fargo's suburban sister and one of the fastest-growing communities in the state, welcomed its first brewery.

Flatland Brewery debuted in July 2016. Its cozy storefront in a new, mixed-use building is surrounded by restaurants, bars, shops, apartments and a concert venue and sports arena. Just eight years earlier, the entire neighborhood was farm fields.

West Fargo's hometown taproom pays tribute to the region's agricultural heritage with its grain elevator logo. There's a grain elevator art installation on the wall of the taproom, too. It's a pared-down, comfortable space, with blond wood tables and a chalkboard menu above the bar. The seventeen-barrel brewhouse is visible just around the corner. Chances are whoever you see behind the bar or in the brewhouse has a stake in the brewery. Flatland Brewing Company is owned and operated by four active brewers and two silent partners who found one another through a web of work, family and homebrewing connections.

It all started when Frank Clemens and Chris Markwardt decided to homebrew together during a business trip for the agricultural implement company they both worked for. They joked about starting a brewery but didn't seriously consider it until Dennis Markwardt (Chris's dad) tried their beer one Christmas and offered an initial investment to get a brewery started. Clemens asked his childhood friend and homebrewing collaborator Aaron Chapman to join the project. Chapman recruited Taylor Nelson, his coworker at a Fargo social services organization and a fellow homebrewer. Dennis Markwardt brought in his college buddy, homebrewer and retired Grand Forks chemist Jeff Thompson.

Chapman, Clemens, Chris Markwardt and Nelson have all kept their day jobs for now (although Clemens is just part time) and arrange their schedules to accommodate the many tasks their new business requires. You'll find all four men brewing beer, serving customers, cleaning out the tanks, ordering merchandise and organizing supplies.

There are a lot of brewers in the Flatland brewhouse, which translates into a varied beer list and an equally diverse clientele. "One of the biggest comments we get is the variety of beers we have on tap," he said. "We've definitely got people who come in and their normal drink is Miller or Bud Light or Busch Light. And then we have people in with their beer tasting books. We've had people in who have been twenty-one for four days, and we've had people who are in their nineties."

Variety will always be a priority for the brewers at Flatland. "Craft beer drinkers who are more into it definitely like trying new things, so we don't want to be so large that we lose that flexibility and can't create more types of beer in smaller batches," Clemens said.

They're casking portions of many of those batches, infusing their American pale ale with oranges and honey and their stout with vanilla and the Minnesota-made maple syrup used in their maple cream soda. An Irish-style red ale and a balanced IPA may be Flatland's best sellers, but the brewers make an effort to create varieties that inspire them. They've zeroed in on subtle, balanced, single-hop, single-malt smash beers and are infusing them with everything from honey to cucumber.

They're also looking to the past, reviving a medieval roggenbier (which is like a super light-bodied hefeweizen made with rye instead of wheat), brewing a classic cream ale and playing around with a holiday brown ale with a spice blend inspired by the pfeffernüsse cookies Clemens's grandma served at Christmas.

The brewery is currently using a 3-barrel brewing system with five ninety-three-gallon fermenters and two double-batch 186-barrel fermenters.

Flatland Brewery's five-year plan includes expanding that capacity and eventually distributing as the brewery grows.

For now, just a few months into their latest brewing experiment, Clemens is content to win over the neighborhood, beer by beer. "When many people walk in, they think we're a bar," he said. "They don't realize that we're a brewery. It starts a conversation about beer."

The Western Pioneers: StoneHome Brewing Company (Watford City), 2016, STONEHOMEBREWING.COM

When brewmaster Kenny Driggers reported for his first day of work at StoneHome Brewing Company in October 2016, he had a lot in common with the brewers who arrived in Dakota Territory before statehood. Like his nineteenth-century predecessors, Driggers was a new North Dakota resident who trained at other commercial breweries before moving to North Dakota.

The Greenville, South Carolina native started volunteering his time at Thomas Creek Brewery during his last semester at Clemson University and took an assistant brewer job there after he graduated. He worked in the industry for seven years before getting the head brewer gig at North Dakota's newest brewery. But he's been brewing beer a lot longer. Driggers first started helping his dad bottle beer at the tender age of ten and even kept it up in his dorm room.

The city Driggers now calls home also has a lot in common with the pre-statehood boomtowns in Dakota Territory. StoneHome Brewing Company is located in Watford City, a small town in the northwestern corner of North Dakota, deep in the heart of North Dakota oil country. City planners there are balancing the needs of established farm and ranch families with those of an influx of mostly male oil field workers and newly arrived young families, while oil prices fluctuate and competition for resources (including housing) remains intense. Integrating newcomers in boom times and weathering a bust are challenges the city fathers in the 1880s would recognize.

The team at the helm of StoneHome Brewing Company knows the market well and is an established player in the western North Dakota bar and restaurant scene. The Watford City brewpub is owned and managed by Six Shooter LLC, which operates several other properties, including Outlaws Bar and Grill in Watford City and Williston, a JL Beers franchise in Watford City and Meadowlark Public House just across the border in Sidney, Montana.

StoneHome's sleek taproom and spacious patio attracted beer fans even before the first test batches of Driggers's beer hit their glasses in December 2016. (A variety of tempting wood-fired pizzas topped with everything from ricotta and figs to a drizzle of North Dakota honey and addictive pub food appetizers certainly helped.)

A red ale and an IPA will be on two of the brewery's tap lines to start. A Norwegian lager, vanilla porter and Berliner weisse are seasonal possibilities. Driggers plans to try a coffee-infused pale ale and a Bavarian wheat beer that will feature local fruit like chokecherries or juneberries. "I'm not trying to create a new category of beer," said Driggers. "I just want to brew the best beer I can to style and then put my own unique spin to it. You can add rainbows and sunshine to a bad beer and it's still going to be bad."

The brewery's final beer list will marry Watford City's drinkers' current favorites and North Dakota craft beer fans' wish lists, which managing partner Angie Pelton describes as "easy-drinking" and "experimental,"

The brewhouse at StoneHome Brewing Company. *Kenny Driggers.*

respectively. StoneHome's fifteen-barrel brewing system, five fifteen-barrel fermenters and two fifteen-barrel brite tanks offer room to experiment and enough capacity to distribute beer to Six Shooter Hospitality's other properties and into North Dakota and eastern Montana.

Western North Dakota craft beer fans can also look for taproom events like beer bingo, beer pairing dinners and an Oktoberfest celebration, as well as bicycle tours that take drinkers to Watford City's craft beer hot spots. Western North Dakota has long been influenced by the craft beer of eastern Montana, and StoneHome Brewing Company is poised to bridge the two brewing communities. Many of StoneHome's customers will come from areas in the western part of that state that currently consider a Montana brewpub to be their hometown brewery.

THE OUTSIDE INFLUENCE: BEAVER CREEK BREWERY (WIBAUX, MONTANA), 2008, BEAVERCREEKBREWERY.COM

Sandon Stinnett and Jim Devine have been brewing beer in tiny Wibaux, Montana (population 461), since 2008. Beaver Creek Brewery beers are available in several North Dakota cities, including Williston, Dickinson and Bismarck. But the closer you get to the Montana border, the more Beaver Creek beer you'll find. "We used to say that we're a regional brewery for all those little towns up and down western North Dakota and eastern Montana," said Devine.

Beaver Creek Brewery operates a taproom and adjacent restaurant/live music venue called the Gem Theatre and Pub in a charming old building in downtown Wibaux. The ingredients in the restaurant's pizza, sandwiches and salads are organic whenever possible, and the menu features fresh bread made with spent grain from the brewery.

The brewery's espresso-tinged Paddlefish Stout, bold Rusty Beaver Wheat and Wibaux's Gold ale are big sellers. But to get a taste of the high-gravity beer Devine's really excited about, you'll have to come to the taproom.

"I set out to build a huge beer, with big beer taste and lots of malt," said Devine. "We knew that by building a big beer, you're going to get big alcohol." That's because high-gravity beer has lots of fermentable and unfermentable materials in the wort for the yeast to eat, and more food for the yeast means more alcohol. Montana breweries can't distribute anything higher than 10 percent

ABV, so strong beer fans will need to make a pilgrimage to try Beaver Creek's biggest beers.

While you're there, don't forget to take a photo by the sign out front. Beaver Creek Brewery came by its name innocently enough (Beaver Creek runs near Wibaux), but its motto ("Our beaver tastes better") is the cheekiest in the region, hands down.

Devine estimates that he's currently brewing one thousand barrels a year on a ten-barrel system but plans to increase production and add a canning line by 2020. The brewery also plans to expand its distribution footprint to the south and west. While Beaver Creek Brewery refines its niche and eyes new competitors in North Dakota and increased competition from western Montana breweries, another brewery on North Dakota's eastern border bridges the brewing philosophies of North Dakota and Minnesota.

The Mad Scientists: Junkyard Brewing Company (Mooorhead, MN), 2012, JUNKYARDBEER.COM

A coconut brown ale that tastes like a candy bar? Check. A spicy Belgian-style quadrupel ale with one of the highest ABV percentages in the Fargo-Moorhead Metro Area? Check. (It's 10.2 ABV, if you're counting.) A super hoppy English IPA inspired by a foraging hippie/hipster buddy? Check. Welcome to Junkyard Brewing Company, the scrappy, DIY beer workshop that's turning out some of the Red River Valley's most experimental beer. (The beers mentioned here are Big Kahuna, Free Candy and Prairie Shaman, if you're curious.)

Brothers Aaron and Dan Juhnke founded their nanobrewery in 2012. They designed and built their own "50-gallon, stainless steel, all-grain brewing system with a custom jacketed brewkettle heated by a couple of 200,000 BTU propane burners" (according to the Junkyard website). They brewed in the back room of Country Cannery on First Avenue North in Moorhead (which sells wine and beer brewing equipment and is owned by early Prairie Homebrewing Companion member Roy Stroh) in the spring of 2013. Moorhead and Fargo have shared a customer base since before statehood (and currently share both a chamber of commerce and a visitors' bureau), so North Dakota drinkers quickly adopted Junkyard as a hometown taproom.

The brewery outgrew that location and moved a few blocks east to the present taproom, where it threw open the garage doors to the patio in the summer of 2014. It's been there ever since, serving beer every night of the week. There are no flagship beers and no long-term plans for widespread distribution, just regular experimental beer releases and a steady stream of live music. Aaron Juhnke, a longtime homebrewer and organizer of the Rare Beer Picnic, wants to keep it that way.

He sees Junkyard Brewing Company as a gateway between the North Dakota and Minnesota brewing worlds, both in philosophy and location. "We probably have more in common with the Minnesota scene," he said. "I think the North Dakota scene tends to be producing more approachable beers and tends to be a bit more focused on having flagships and the old-school production model." But, he added, "We definitely kind of align more with the North Dakota brewers in terms of industry relationship." Junkyard Brewing Company is a member of both the Minnesota Craft Brewers Guild and the North Dakota Brewers Guild.

The brewery tripled its capacity in 2016, adding a 10-barrel system to increase production from the 350 to 400 barrels produced in 2016 to 800 to 1,000 barrels a year. Junkyard Brewing Company's small, agile, experimental brewing philosophy fills a niche for North Dakota customers.

A mix of production breweries, brewpubs and retail-focused taprooms gives North Dakota beer fans more options than ever. The competition challenges breweries to be both creative and strategic. Yet the beer scene is still small enough to retain the spirit of collaboration that sparked the craft beer explosion in the first place. There are currently more breweries selling locally brewed, North Dakota beer than at any time in history. And still more are on the way. The third North Dakota beer boom isn't done yet.

Chapter 7

WHAT'S NEXT

New Players, Expanded Distribution and Local Pride

Good people drink good beer.
—*Hunter S. Thompson*

While the national craft brewing industry hits its stride, the craft beer scene in North Dakota is still growing. Local brewers are carving out a niche for their products within the state, across the Upper Midwest and into the prairie provinces of Canada. They're doing it the same way that brewers have done it here since before statehood—saturating the local and regional markets, showcasing homegrown talent and ingredients and drinking with their neighbors. New breweries are bringing local beer to neighborhoods that have never had a taproom.

THE TRADITIONALIST: PRAIRIE BROTHERS BREWING COMPANY (FARGO), 2016
PRAIRIEBROTHERSBREWING.COM

Prairie Brothers Brewing Company was established in 2016 and opened in April 2017. Its southwest Fargo location is part of a recent shift toward opening taprooms in established retail locations instead of industrial parks or downtown entertainment districts. It's the third brewery in a neighborhood that's bisected by I-94, which draws travelers from Minnesota to the east and Montana to the west. Fargo Brewing Company's Ale House opened off the same exit in the fall of 2016. Flatland Brewing Company is located one exit west, in West Fargo.

Prairie Brothers Brewing Company owner and brewmaster Don Kenna and taproom manager Wil Petick wanted a minimal, rustic interior to keep the attention on the beer, the local art on the walls and the musicians on stage. "With the prairie theme, we're looking at keeping it very simple," said Kenna. "We just want to have that local, neighborhood bar feeling."

The beer list is equally streamlined, but that doesn't mean the selections aren't complex. Kenna and Petick are both homebrewers, and the beer in the taproom is inspired by their collaborations and the beer that Kenna (a former science teacher) loved researching and perfecting (and drinking, of course). "We're focusing really on English styles like the English bitters, maybe some of the Scottish ales and doing more of a traditional take," Kenna said. "We'd like to stick with the German purity laws with most of the beers." A light and mellow cream ale, a pale ale, a stout and an Irish Red were among the first Prairie Brothers Brewing Company beers available in the taproom.

Prairie Brothers Brewing Company also draws inspiration from its neighbors to the north. A chance meeting with Peg Beer Company in Winnipeg led to a collaboration between the two breweries. "We're talking about doing a Canadian pale ale," said Kenna. "We're gonna put our own little twist on it and promote a little Canadian brotherhood. It's something we haven't seen a lot of, and hopefully we can develop a little niche."

Prairie Brothers Brewing Company merchandise was ready before the brewery was completed. *Don Kenna.*

Kenna estimates that Prairie Brothers will eventually produce one thousand barrels a year. The brewery will self-distribute to start, with a possible second location and canning facility in the five-year plan. But for now, it's focusing on taproom sales and seeing how the neighborhood and its tastes evolve.

Breweries like Prairie Brothers reach residents who had previously lived far from a local taproom, but they also pull drinkers out of the chain restaurants and hotel bars that draw thousands of regional travelers to the West Acres shopping district nearby. Targeting casual beer drinkers and tourists is a new idea for North Dakota breweries, but putting breweries in the cities' hottest development zones has already attracted new craft beer fans.

The close-knit beer scene and word of mouth are already creating a little buzz among beer nerds. North Dakota isn't exactly a beercation hot spot just yet, but if a craft beer fan walks into any taproom or craft beer bar in the state, the small, chummy beer community will totally hook them up with a list of places (and beers) to try next.

Laughing Sun's Mike Frohlich loves to tell the tale of two Canadian couples that took a crazy detour to visit his Bismarck brewery en route to a Winnipeg beer festival. "They found out about us and drove from Fargo to Bismarck and back to get some beers, pint glasses and a couple of growlers," he said. That's just under four hundred miles round trip.

The Wild Card: Drumconrath Brewing Company (Mapleton), 2016
DRUMCONRATHBREWING.COM

Drumconrath Brewing Company in Mapleton is testing just how off the beaten path craft beer nerds are willing to go. When the doors opened in 2017, it was the only craft brewery in North Dakota located in a small North Dakota town. There hasn't been a brewery in a community of fewer than one thousand people since Dunseith's Turtle Mountain Brewery closed just after statehood.

It helps that Mapleton is a quick, twenty-minute drive west of most neighborhoods in Fargo-Moorhead and located right off busy I-94. Owner and brewer Sam Corr hopes that the novelty of his business will encourage beer fans and travelers to stop. His brewery is unusual, both in theme and location.

The 2,160-square-foot, white corrugated steel building isn't fancy, but there's just enough room to squeeze the three-barrel brewing system, with its eight fermenters and two seven-barrel brite tanks, behind the bar and still have space for seating and a pool table. Corr's betting that the easygoing atmosphere and rural location will appeal to "country guys" like himself. After the brewery construction was finished, "I stood in the doorway and looked out," he said with a grin. "There's *nothing*." His smile is so big you can hear it in his voice.

An early Drumconrath Brewing Company sign from before the brewery settled in Mapleton. *Sam Corr.*

The space inside Drumconrath Brewing Company is a tribute to one of Corr's other passions, Ireland. He named his brewery for the town in Ireland where his ancestors lived, Irish flags hang in the taproom and Drumconrath's motto, *Bród agus díograis*, means "Pride and passion" in Irish. He's even planning to brew an old-style Irish farmhouse ale with dark, smoked malt and wild yeast harvested from honey from the brewery's namesake Irish village. St. Patrick's Day is obviously going to be a really big deal at Drumconrath Brewing Company. Look for Corr's St. Patrick's Day Marchtoberfest, a traditional Oktoberfest style every spring.

Corr learned about beer from his mentor, Pugs Hayes at Hayes' Public House in Buffalo, Minnesota, and developed forty beer recipes as a homebrewer. Drumconrath Brewing Company features a handful of year-round beers, like Gale Force West Coast American Style IPA, an Irish stout and Ribbon Man Red, as well as a series of seasonals. Most of Corr's base malt is from Two Track Malting Company.

He prefers all-malt, traditional styles with one major (and unique) exception: he's also planning an entirely gluten-free line of beer. "Many use an enzyme in the mash to break down gluten, but instead of doing that and risking having that contamination, I'm going to use the ancient grains," Corr explained. His gluten-free IPA, red and porter will use millet and buckwheat instead of barley.

Drumconrath Brewing Company will brew 150 to 200 barrels a year for the first year and self-distribute to start. Corr's five-year plan includes expanding to a larger brewing system and distributing throughout the region.

WHAT'S ON TAP

More breweries, new ingredients and a more informed and adventurous clientele mean that there are more beer styles available in North Dakota right now than at any time in history. Historically, beer fans here drank a large amount of just a few beer styles—ale in the frontier forts, lager and Vienna-style wiener beer before statehood and then lots of light lagers during Prohibition and for decades after. The craft beer fans in the '90s loved easy-drinking amber and pale ales, but drinkers in modern North Dakota are up for anything.

"We recognize that craft beer drinkers are promiscuous," said Drekker Brewing Company's Mark Bjornstad. "It's not like when you picked your beer, your smokes and your car and that was your life. Craft beer drinkers want variety."

"When the Great Northern opened, it was absolutely necessary to have a light crossover beer available for those who were unfamiliar or afraid of craft beer," said Dick Nilles. "That isn't really the case anymore. Beer tastes in North Dakota have expanded vastly over the past twenty years."

North Dakota brewers are offering plenty of variety, moving away from the ales and IPAs that launched their businesses and reviving older European beer styles, shifting toward subtle, balanced beers and appealing to wine drinkers with a range of sour beers. A renewed focus on malt-forward styles is good news for barley producers, maltsters and anyone who enjoys a rich, malty pint.

MORE BEER, MORE PLACES

The primary sales territory for local breweries hasn't changed much since before statehood; North Dakota and the surrounding states of Minnesota, South Dakota and Montana still make up the main market for North Dakota–made beer. Fargo Brewing Company will be the first North Dakota craft brewery to distribute its products internationally when it expands into Manitoba in 2017.

Every brewery in the state plans to increase production, so the North Dakota beer market will look very different after 2021. The largest production breweries in the state all project an increase over the next five years. Fargo Brewing Company is shooting for 10,000 barrels a year, Drekker Brewing Company 3,000 and Rhombus Guys Brewing Company 3,500.

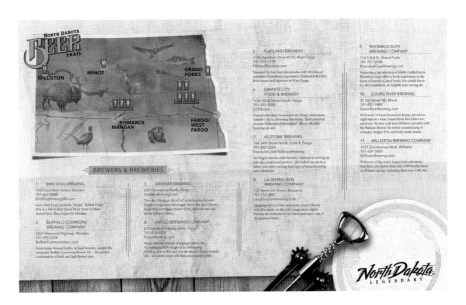

The State of North Dakota actively promotes beer hotspots. Note: Williston Brewing Company does not brew onsite. *North Dakota Tourism.*

The retail-focused brewpubs and taprooms plan to ramp up production as well. Laughing Sun Brewing Company wants to reach 3,000 barrels a year by 2021, Buffalo Commons Brewing Company 1,800, Bird Dog Brewing 200 and Souris River Brewing 1,500. The two 2017 newcomers estimate a combined minimum output of 1,200 annually.

Even with just nine of North Dakota's twelve breweries reporting (and estimating low, in some cases), that still puts 2021 projections just over 24,000 barrels of beer per year—an almost threefold increase over 2015's total of 8,452. Add in the remaining three craft beer companies, the breweries that are rumored to be in the planning stages across the state and the one confirmed newcomer to the Fargo brewing scene slated to arrive in 2017–18, and the forecast for North Dakota beer production looks bright.

Farm to Table Comes Full Circle

Those numbers are modest compared to some craft brewing states, but for most North Dakota brewers and craft beer fans, it's never really been a volume game. This is a state with just under 760,000 people, after all. We don't expect to be the biggest or the most popular. In fact, we kind of like being the scrappy underdog, and we're used to flying under the radar. People here appreciate folks who can roll up their sleeves and create something tangible. That includes beer. And that beer is going back to its roots and using more local ingredients than ever.

North Dakota farmers continue to supply the malting barley to the biggest national breweries, as well as the fast-growing craft beer market. Local craft maltster Two Track Malting Company will never malt as much as the big boys at Rahr, Cargill and Anheuser-Busch, but it offers a hyper-local alternative to brewers who want to brew beer from North Dakota ingredients. Two Track Malting Company plans to produce thirty tons of malt a week by 2020, opening up new opportunities for North Dakota farmers and brewers.

If Two Track wants to expand the craft malting industry in North Dakota, Fargo Brewing Company brewer Chris Anderson wants to redefine it. Anderson partnered with Appareo Systems in Fargo to create a scaled-down, automated version of malting equipment that would allow barley farmers and small malters to malt their own barley and sell directly to breweries. The project was unveiled in 2016 and may reach the market in 2017.

Producers of hops in North Dakota are already selling directly to breweries. Until recently, only whole-cone hops were available. But Jamie Good, local foods specialist for the North Dakota Department of Agriculture, thinks that the appearance of the first pelletizer in the state at Ostlie's Sunnyside Acres near Carrington in 2016 just might be a game-changer.

This pelletizer converts dried hops into small pellets that can be stored much more easily than sticky, messy, whole-cone hops. It makes local hops available to all breweries, not just those with brewing equipment that can accommodate whole-cone hops. If more farmers invest in a pelletizer (or contract with an operation that has one), Good thinks that hops production in the state could expand to twenty acres very quickly. That's nothing in terms of overall acreage, but it would make hops available to the breweries that want them. Brewer demand for North Dakota hops is so strong that hops farmers can currently sell their entire crop to just one brewery to make one beer. Some brewers source or supplement with additional hops from farmers' market vendors or friends who grow them in their yards. Most of these hops aren't included in the total Department of Agriculture count.

Kyla Splichal, horticulture research specialist at North Dakota State University, thinks that twenty acres might be too high. But the variety trials she and Harlene Hatterman-Valenti completed in 2016 give farmers (and brewers) valuable data about how twelve varieties of hops (Cascade,

Harvesting hops at Ostlie's Sunnyside Acres. *Lindsay Ostlie.*

Centennial, Challenger, Brewer's Gold, Galena, Glacier, Mt. Hood, Newport, Nugget, Willamette, Spalt Select and Zeus) fared in North Dakota. The study might get farmers outside the state's craft brewing community talking about a crop most aren't familiar with.

Brewer experimentation opens up more opportunities for sourcing supplementary ingredients, like honey, berries, pumpkins and apples. Local pride is what craft brewing in North Dakota is all about. North Dakota beer fans just want more good, readily available, farm-to-table beer with that local connection.

It's a warm autumn night in Bismarck. As darkness falls, Laughing Sun Brewing Company's taproom fills up, and patrons spill out onto the sidewalk patio. There is no way to drink in this space without getting cozy, no way to chat without bending your head closer to your companion. Friends scoot closer to strangers on the long, shared banquette. One couple, handsomely dressed and telling stories of their grown children, moves toward brewer Mike Frohlich in order to accommodate the growing crowd. The three sit and chat a while, discussing the beer, the couple's last visit and their hopes for the neighborhood.

Frohlich surveys the table with a grin. This, he explains, is what he loves about making beer in North Dakota. He loves the taproom atmosphere, the connection with his customers and the fact that his suppliers pop in the back door and say hello. He taps the half-empty glass in front of him, the one that contains the beer he brewed with barley grown and malted by his buddies and flavored with berries grown in a nearby town—the official beer of the community's Oktoberfest celebration. "This is a glass of relationships to me," he said. "It's kind of a synergy of all of these things."

HAVE A DRINK WITH US

If you've made it to the end of this book, then you know the only thing North Dakotans like more than a beer is a good party. Here are a few of the best and longest-running craft beer events from around the state.

ONGOING

SEASONAL COTEAU DES PRAIRIES LODGE BEER DINNERS
cdplodge.com
Havana

Local chefs and brewers serve up multi-course food and beer pairings during quarterly beer dinners held in a rustic chic dining room with an endless view. Sometimes they even brew using hops grown on the family farm.

APRIL

BACON AND BEER FESTIVAL
baconandbeerfargo.com
Fargo

The largest beer sampling event in the region offers beer from about one hundred vendors and bacon-infused dishes from dozens of local restaurants. It's a must for any beer or bacon fiend.

JUNE

UNDER BREW SKIES
underbrewskies.com
Fargo

Sample craft beer from North Dakota breweries and a total of sixty other independent beer makers at this outdoor beer festival in downtown Fargo's Island Park. It's hosted by the North Dakota Brewers Guild.

JULY

ZOO BREW
redriverzoo.org
Fargo

A ticket to Zoo Brew at the Red River Zoo gets you zoo admission, beer from local breweries and pubs, live music, lawn games and up-close animal encounters.

THE RARE BEER PICNIC
junkyardbeer.com/rare-beer-picnic
Moorhead, MN

This outdoor sampling event in Davy Park is co-hosted by the chefs at Usher's House and brewers at Junkyard Brewing Company. It features aged, soured and infused beers from local breweries and homebrewers from both Minnesota and North Dakota.

SEPTEMBER

MANDAN OKTOBERFEST
mandanprogress.org
Mandan

This all-ages community festival features German food, music, kids' activities and a beer garden with dozens of beers, including offerings from the local craft breweries in the community.

OCTOBER

KEGS AND CANVAS: ART AND ALE WALK
downtownfargo.com
Fargo

Stroll downtown Fargo and watch artists at work as you sample beer from local restaurants, bars and craft breweries.

MUDDY RIVER MASHERS OKTOBERFEST
facebook.com/MuddyRiverMashers
Bismarck

The Muddy River Mashers Homebrew Club hosts an Oktoberfest party that features beers from both homebrewers and local breweries. There's food and a chance to rock your traditional German outfits, too.

THE PRAIRIE HOMEBREWING COMPANION HOPPY HALLOWEEN CONTEST AND BANQUET
hoppyhalloween.com
Fargo

Any homebrewer in the United States or Canada can enter a beer in this annual contest, which has been held in Fargo since the mid-'90s. The best beers out of hundreds of entries are announced at a celebratory banquet.

NOVEMBER

THE PIG AND THE PINT
baconandbeerfargo.com
Fargo

Local restaurants have a week to prepare half a hog and collaborate with local breweries to create unique beer and food pairings. It's a semiformal bash that offers a VIP experience and a whole lot of food.

LEARN TO HOMEBREW DAY
facebook.com/MuddyRiverMashers
Bismarck

The homebrewers of the Muddy River Mashers homebrew club teach their friends, family and neighbors how to brew their own beer during this annual event. This event is appropriate for brewers of every skill level.

FARGO BREWER'S BALL
cfanorthdakota.com
Fargo

Try craft beer from North Dakota breweries, as well as wine and spirits, food and live music. The proceeds from the event help fund research for cystic fibrosis.

BIBLIOGRAPHY

Ackley, Warren. Personal interview, October 4, 2016.

Anderson, Chris. E-mail interview, April 12, 2017.

Anderson, Ryan. "Fargo's Great Northern Closes." MNbeer.com. http://mnbeer.com/2005/10/06/fargos-great-northern-closes.

Beer Advocate. "Yeast Guide." https://www.beeradvocate.com/beer/101/yeast.

The Beer Professor. "Vienna." http://www.thebeerprofessor.com/?tag=wiener-lager.

Benjamin H. Barrett Papers, MS 255. Institute for Regional Studies, North Dakota State University, Fargo.

Berg, Francie, M., ed. *Ethnic Heritage in North Dakota*. Washington, D.C.: Attiyeh Foundation, 1983.

A Bicentennial History of Devils Lake, North Dakota. Devils Lake, ND: The Committee, 1976.

Bismarck Tribune. December 12, 1997.

———. February 4, 1996.

Bjorke, Christopher. "Beer Plans a'Brewin' in Bismarck-Mandan." *Bismarck Tribune*, January 31, 2010. http://bismarcktribune.com/business/local/beer-plans-a-brewin-in-bismarck-mandan/article_d717450e-0c67-11df-96a9-001cc4c002e0.html.

Bjornstad, Mark. Personal interview, July 21, 2014.

———. Phone interview, October 26, 2016.

Blank, Fallon, and Grant Wigen. Personal interview, November 22, 2016.

Breker, Joe. Phone interview, October 27, 2016.

Breker, Phil. E-mail interviews, October 7, 13, 2016.

Brewers Association. "History of Craft Brewing." https://www.brewersassociation.org/brewers-association/history/history-of-craft-brewing.

———. "North Dakota Craft Beer Statistics 2015." https://www.brewersassociation.org/statistics/by-state/?state=ND.

———. "Number of Breweries." https://www.brewersassociation.org/statistics/number-of-breweries.

Brown, Dee. *Bury My Heart at Wounded Knee: An Indian History of the American West.* New York: Henry Holt and Company Inc., 1970.

Butcher, Carole. Personal interview, September 2, 2016.

Carley, Kenneth. *The Dakota War of 1862: Minnesota's Other Civil War.* St. Paul: Minnesota Historical Society Press, 1961.

Clemens, Frank. Personal interview, November 15, 2016.

Corr, Sam. E-mail interview, November 26, 2016.

CraftBeer.com. "Beer History." https://www.craftbeer.com/the-beverage/history-of-beer/the-american-story.

Cree, Maria. Personal interview, September 27, 2016.

Dagman, Dana, and Travis Dagman. Phone interview, October 26, 2016.

Daily Optic. September 8, 1914.

Davis, Jim. "Prohibition Strategy." Prairie Public, May 30, 2014. http://www.prairiepublic.org/radio/dakota-datebook?post=56336.

———. "Republican Triumph." Prairie Public, October 16, 2014. http://www.prairiepublic.org/radio/dakota-datebook?post=56336.

Davison, Kathleen, ed. *North Dakota History: Readings About the Northern Plains State.* Fargo: North Dakota Center for Distance Education, 2008.

Department of Immigration and Statistics. *1887: Resources of Dakota.* N.p., 1887. https://books.google.com/books?id=VX0fAAAAYAAJ&pg=PA455&lpg=PA455&dq=dunseith+%2B+turtle+mountain+brewery&source=bl&ots=gzKF98Npi_&sig=EJgObJmJ1pNc-s0g42v_kC70Tzw&hl=en&sa=X&ved=0ahUKEwjp0tKqvO_QAhUCPiYKHWEoBocQ6AEIRzAI#v=onepage&q=dunseith%20%2B%20turtle%20mountain%20brewery&f=false.

Devine, Jim. Phone interview, October 26, 2016.

Diegal, Violet. Personal interview, March 13, 2017.

Domaskin, Andrea. "Great Northern's Closure Leaves Barrels of Beer, Building in Limbo. InForum, October 7, 2005. http://www.inforum.com/content/great-northerns-closure-leaves-barrels-beer-building-limbo.

Donovan, Lauren. "40th Anniversary of Infamous Zip to Zap Party Nears." *Bismarck Tribune*, May 9, 2009. http://bismarcktribune.com/news/local/th-anniversary-of-infamous-zip-to-zap-party-nears/article_d2f0dc9a-85ac-533d-8431-b2f34360906e.html.

Driggers, Kenny. E-mail interviews, October 25, November 17–18, 2016.

Eccher, Marino. "North Dakota Brewery on Tap." InForum, October 9, 2010. http://www.inforum.com/content/north-dakota-brewery-tap.

Edwinton Brewing Company Facebook Page. https://www.facebook.com/EdwintonBrewing/?fref=ts.

Eidbo, Carl. E-mail interview, December 15, 2016.

Engelhardt, Carroll. *Gateway to the Northern Plains: Railroads and the Birth of Fargo and Moorhead*. Minneapolis: University of Minnesota Press, 2007.

Eriksmoen, Curt. "Mondak, a Drinking Man's Oasis in Dry North Dakota." *Bismarck Tribune*, June 20, 2015. http://bismarcktribune.com/news/columnists/curt-eriksmoen/mondak-a-drinking-man-s-oasis-in-dry-north-dakota/article_39f51526-88a0-5058-bd24-4b5cdb8f8e32.html.

Fargo, North Dakota: Its History and Images. "Great Northern Railway Depot." https://library.ndsu.edu/fargo-history/?q=content/great-northern-railway-depot.

Fehr, Kris. *Bismarck Tribune*. August 18, 1996.

———. *Bismarck Tribune*. August 14, 1995

———. *Bismarck Tribune*. February 26, 1995.

Feist, Sarah. "Bird Dog Brewing." *Feisty Eats*, May 21, 2015. https://feistyeats.wordpress.com/2015/05/21/bird-dog-brewing.

FM Greeter. "Local Breweries." November 1997.

Frank E. Vyzralek, MSS 10553. Sub-Series II: Beer and Bottling, Boxes 9-11. State Historical Society of North Dakota, Bismarck, North Dakota. September 28, 2016.

Frank, J.W., R.S. Moore and G.M. Ames. "Historical and Cultural Roots of Drinking Problems Among American Indians." *American Journal of Public Health* 90, no. 3 (2000): 344–51.

Frohlich, Mike. Personal interview, September 28. 2016.

Gilman, Carolyn, and Mary Jane Schneider. *The Way to Independence: Memories of a Hidatsa Indian Family, 1840–1920*. St. Paul: Minnesota Historical Press, 1987.

Good, Jamie. Phone interview, September 21, 2016.

Granlund, Royce. Personal interview, October 27, 2016.

Grundberg, Dean. "Laughing Sun Grand Opening." FM Beer. http://www.fmbeer.com/events/laughing-sun-grand-opening.

————. E-mail interview, December 15, 2016.

Guerrero, John, William C. Sherman and Paul L. Whitney. *Prairie Peddlers: The Syrian-Lebanese in North Dakota*. Bismarck, ND: University of Mary Press, 2002.

Gunderson, Chad. Phone interview, October 28, 2016.

Hageman, John. "With Rhombus Guys Brewpub Opening, Historic Opera House Comes to Life." *Grand Forks Herald*, September 26, 2015. http://www.grandforksherald.com/news/local/3847689-rhombus-guys-brewpub-opening-historic-opera-house-comes-life.

Halgrimson, Andrea. "Historic Depot Up for Grabs." InForum, October 7, 2006. http://www.inforum.com/content/historic-depot-grabs.

Hart, Arthur. "'Hurdy-Gurdy' Girls Danced with Lonely Men—for a Fee." *Idaho Statesman*, June 6, 2006. http://www.idahostatesman.com/news/state/idaho/history/article40683693.html.

Helgeson, Charlotte. Personal interview, August 28, 2016.

Helm, Merry. "Beer and Bloodshed." Prairie Public, October 18, 2005. http://www.prairiepublic.org/radio/dakota-datebook?post=4794.

————. "Capone in East Grand Forks." Prairie Public, May 24, 2011. http://www.prairiepublic.org/radio/dakota-datebook?post=31856.

Hendricks, Arron. Phone interview, April 17, 2017.

Herzog, Karen. "North Dakota's Heritage of Alcohol." *Bismarck Tribune*, December 9, 2012. http://bismarcktribune.com/news/state-and-regional/north-dakota-s-heritage-of-alcohol/article_6fd6cc22-3fca-11e2-ad03-001a4bcf887a.html.

Hill, Aaron. Personal interview, September 6, 2013.

————. Phone interview, September 28, 2016.

Historical and Cultural Society of Clay County. *The Historic Breweries of Fargo-Moorhead*. Moorhead, MN: self-published, n.d.

Hoffback, Dr. Steve. "Bismarck's Breweries of the 1870s and 1880s." Prairie Public, July 18, 2016. http://www.prairiepublic.org/radio/dakota-datebook/page/6?post=66872.

Hoffman, Randy. "Edwinton Brewing Launches Local Beer at Peacock Alley." Bismarckcafe.com, October 19, 2012. http://www.bismarckcafe.com/blogs/7423/edwinton-brewing-launches-local-beer-at-peacock-alley.

Hoffman, Ted. Phone interview, October 27. 2016.

Holdman, Jessica. "Brewer Seeking Location." *Bismarck Tribune*, March 11, 2012. http://bismarcktribune.com/news/columnists/jessica-holdman/brewer-seeking-location/article_d4627336-6941-11e1-9ccc-001871e3ce6c.html.

Horsley, Dr. Richard. Phone interview, November 10, 2016.

Hoverson, Doug. *Amber Waters: The History of Brewing in Minnesota*. Minneapolis: University of Minnesota Press, 2007.

Indie GoGo. "Little Deep Beer Company." https://www.indiegogo.com/projects/little-deep-beer-company.

Ingrsoll, Archie. "Privy Shaft a Window to Brothel's Past." *Grand Forks Herald*, August 20, 2016. http://www.grandforksherald.com/news/4098581-privy-shaft-window-brothels-past.

Jamestown Sun. "When Times Were Dry." June 9, 2008. http://www.jamestownsun.com/content/when-times-were-dry.

Jantzi, Darin. "News Release: National Agricultural Statistics Service." USDA, June 30, 2016. https://www.nass.usda.gov/Statistics_by_State/North_Dakota/Publications/Crops_and_Stocks/2016/ND_acg1606.pdf.

Johnson, Mary Ann. Phone interview, October 7, 2016.

Juhnke, Aaron. Phone interview, October 27, 2016.

Junkyard Brewing Company. http://www.junkyardbeer.com.

Kaugenberg, Brian. "Now Open (Or Damn Close): Drekker Brewing." *The Growler*, August 4, 2014. http://growlermag.com/now-open-or-damn-close-drekker-brewing.

Kenna, Don. Personal interview, October 6, 2016.

Knutson, Gertrude. "When Will Rogers Said Moorhead Was 'the Wickedest City in the World.'" In *It Really Happened Here!: Amazing Tales of Minnesota and The Dakotas*. Edited by Ethelyn Pearson and Steve Tweed. Fargo, ND: McLeery & Sons Publishing, 2000.

Kolpack, Dave. Associated Press, January 25, 2013. https://www.yahoo.com/news/nd-bill-allow-brew-pubs-233427886.html?ref=gs.

Kopp, Craig. Phone interview, October 4, 2016.

Kramer, Paul. Phone interview, November 8, 2016.

Krueger, Markus. "Blind Pigs, Bootleggers, and the Birth of Bars." History on Tap, Junkyard Brewing Company, Moorhead, Minnesota, April 3, 2017.

———. Personal interview, November 29, 2016.

Kwandt, Dennis. Phone interview, December 6, 2016.

Lakoduk, Jon. Phone interview, August 23, 2016.

Lamb, John. "Beer Brewing." *High Plains Reader*, July 3, 1997.

Larson, Troy. "Ghost Town: Mondak, Montana." Ghosts of North Dakota, February 7, 2016. http://www.ghostsofnorthamerica.com/ghost-town-mondak-montana.

Lascity, Ethan. "North Dakota Is the Beer Drinking Capital Of America." *International Business Times*, June, 30, 2015. http://www.ibtimes.com/pulse/north-dakota-beer-drinking-capital-america-1990553.

Legends of America. "Old West Legends: Painted Ladies of the Old West." http://www.legendsofamerica.com/we-paintedlady.html.

Lukens, Fred. Phone interview, October 27, 2016.

Mandan Historical Society. "The Battle with 'the Bottle.'" http://www.mandanhistory.org/areahistory/prohibitioninmandan.html.

Marsh, Bernie, and Paulette Marsh. Phone interview, December 13, 2015.

Martin, Michael, J. "Vice and Violence in Ward County, North Dakota, 1905–1920." MS thesis, University of North Dakota, 1977.

McQuade, Sam W. *There Is a Road in North Dakota: Memoirs of a Dakota Budman.* Bismarck, ND: Sam W. McQuade, 2010.

Meyers, Augustus. *Ten Years in the Ranks.* New York: Sterling Press, 1914. Kindle ed.

MHA Nation. "MHA History." http://mhanation.com/main2/history.html.

Minot Daily News. "Adventures 'n Cooking: Daniel Haff Moves from Battlefield to the Kitchen." January 28, 2013. http://content.minotdailynews.com/?p=572749/Adventures--n-cooking--Daniel-Haff-moves-from-battlefield-to-the-kitchen.html.

National Park Service. "The Grandest Fort on the Upper Missouri River." https://www.nps.gov/fous/index.htm.

Native Languages of the Americas. "Assiniboine Indian Fact Sheet." http://www.bigorrin.org/assiniboine_kids.htm.

Nielson, Jade. E-mail interview, March 27, 2017.

Nilles, Dick. E-mail interview, December 16, 2016.

Ostlie, Lindsay. Phone interview, September 26, 2016.

Palmerston, John Robertson. *A Political Manual of the Province of Manitoba and the North-West Territories.* N.p.: Call Printing Company, 1887. https://books.google.com/books?id=hVUvAAAAYAAJ&pg=PA81&lpg=PA81&dq=Edward+L.+Drewry+winnipeg&source=bl&ots=E1dHYO-W3-&sig=B8gGuoRrico_bFJcBm5tVp4OgKo&hl=en&sa=X&ved=0ahUKEwjR2IiGju_PAhVH-mMKHa0YDwEQ6AEINTAF#v=onepage&q&f=false.

Peihl, Mark. Personal interview, November 29, 2016.

Prairie Public. "Milwaukee Brewery Company." November 2, 2008. http://www.prairiepublic.org/radio/dakota-datebook?post=2262.

Rath-Wald, Carmen. Twitter interview, September 29, 2016.

Rementer, Rose. "Beer List Released for Rhombus Guys Brewing Company." *Grand Forks Herald*, August 6, 2015. http://www.grandforksherald.com/news/region/3812476-beer-list-released-rhombus-guys-brewing-company.

Reshaping the Tornado Belt. "Jacob Dobmeier." http://www.reshapingthetornadobelt.com/background/gfk-pioneer-biographies/jacob-dobmeier.

Reuben Liechty Realtors. "Jamestown History." http://www.liechtyrealestate.com/Jamestown/JamestownHistory.

Rickey, Don, Jr. *Forty Miles a Day on Beans and Hay: The Enlisted Soldier Fighting the Indian Wars.* Norman: University of Oklahoma Press, 1963.

Rogers, Jacquie. "The Entertainers: Hurdy Gurdy Girls." *Unusual Historicals,* June 11, 2011. http://unusualhistoricals.blogspot.com/2011/06/entertainers-hurdy-gurdy-girls.html.

Sandstrom, Tessa. "A Dry Brew." Prairie Public, October 16, 2006. http://www.prairiepublic.org/radio/dakota-datebook?post=4012.

Schmidt, Dr. Bryan. Personal interview, September 27, 2016.

Shepard, Harvey. *Oh Beautiful Beer: The Evolution of Craft Beer & Design.* New York: Countryman Press, 2015.

Slater, Alan. Phone interview, November 16, 2016.

Souris River Brewing Facebook Page. https://www.facebook.com/SourisRiverBrewing/?fref=ts.

Splichal, Kyla. Phone interview, September 23, 2016.

Standing Rock Sioux Tribe. http://standingrock.org/history.

State Historical Society of North Dakota. "Pembina State Museum—History." http://history.nd.gov/historicsites/pembina/pembinahistory5.html.

———. "Self-Guided Tour, Former Governors' Mansion State Historic Site." http://history.nd.gov/historicsites/fgm/pdf/FGMTour.pdf.

Stober, Jared. Phone interview, October 4, 2016.

Stutrud, Joshua. Phone interview, October 20, 2016.

Stutrud, Mark. Phone interview, December 8, 2016.

Sylvester, Stephen G. "Avenues for Ladies Only: The Soiled Doves of East Grand Forks, 1887–1915." *Minnesota History Magazine.* http://collections.mnhs.org/MNHistoryMagazine/articles/51/v51i08p291-300.pdf.

Thackery, Lorna. "Booze Lubricated Mondak's Prosperity." Mid-Rivers Communications. http://www.midrivers.com/~fairview/boozel~1.pdf.

Third Annual Report of the State Superintendent of Irrigation and Forestry, Volume 3. Jamestown, ND: Alert, State Printers and Binders, 1894. https://books.google.com/books?id=Z9bNAAAAMAAJ&pg=PA112&lpg=PA112&dq=dunseith+%2B+turtle+mountain+brewery&source=bl&ots=T7JD0HR-FY&sig=KP57ZWGqI3LF28KHv_LaOZBJWPU&hl=en&sa=X&ved=0ahUKEwjp0tKqvO_QAhUCPiYKHWEoBocQ6AEISjAJ#v=onepage&q=dunseith%20%2B%20turtle%20mountain%20brewery&f=false.

Thompson, Aaron. Phone interview, April 12, 2017.

Tolna Tribune. "The Jail Leaked." July 4, 1907.

Tuhy, Dale. Phone interview, December 13, 2016.

Turtle Mountain Star. "Many Pioneer Industries Served People During Territorial Days." June 16, 1932. http://tur.stparchive.com/Archive/TUR/TUR06161932P08.php.

Tweton, D. Jerome, and Everett C. Albers, eds. *The Way It Was: The North Dakota Frontier Experience.* Vol. 6, *The Townspeople.* Fessenden, ND: Grass Roots Press, 2004.

———. *The Way It Was: The North Dakota Frontier Experience.* Vol. 3, *The Cowboys and Ranchers.* Fessenden, ND: Grass Roots Press, 1999.

———. *The Way It Was: The North Dakota Frontier Experience.* Vol. 2, *Norwegian Homesteaders.* Fessenden, ND: Grass Roots Press, 1998.

United States Department of Agriculture. "Acreage." http://www.usda.gov/nass/PUBS/TODAYRPT/acrg0616.pdf.

United States Department of Interior, National Park Service. "National Register of Historic Places Multiple Property Documentation Form." July 25, 1989. http://focus.nps.gov/GetAsset?assetID=c4ec19fc-898f-4c72-ae1e-1c6ff32b715f.

U.S. Census Bureau. "Quick Facts North Dakota." http://www.census.gov/quickfacts/table/PST045216/38.

Weiss, Emily. "Chasing the Beer Scene in the Dakotas." *The Growler*, March 8, 2013. http://growlermag.com/chasing-the-beer-scene-in-the-dakotas.

"Wet and Dry: Alcohol in Clay County, 1871–1937." Historical and Cultural Society of Clay County. 202 First Avenue North, Moorhead, Minnesota, November 29, 2016.

Wheeler, Margaret. Personal interview, April 19, 2017.

Wolfe, Allan. "High Gravity Beer: Big Risk, Bigger Reward." CraftBeer.com. https://www.craftbeer.com/craft-beer-muses/high-gravity-beer-big-risk-bigger-reward.

Workers of the Federal Writers' Project of the Works Progress Administration for the State of North Dakota. *The American Guide Series: North Dakota.* Fargo, ND: Knight Printing Company, 1938.

INDEX

ABOUT THE AUTHOR

Alicia Underlee Nelson is a freelance writer and photographer who covers craft beer, travel, art, entertainment, midwestern history and North Dakota news for Thomson Reuters, *Delta Sky* magazine, *AAA Living* magazine, Matador Network, the Food Network and numerous other travel, news and lifestyle publications. She lives in West Fargo, North Dakota, with her husband and son. Follow her adventures across the Upper Midwest and the prairie provinces of Canada at prairiestylefile.com.